Ghosts of
Portland, Oregon

Todd Cobb

D1301670

Schiffer Publishing Ltd
4880 Lower Valley Road Atglen, Pennsylvania 19310

Other Schiffer Books on Related Subjects
Schiffer Publishing, Ltd. has several books highlighting the ghosts that roam various cities in the United States. Please go to our website to for more information about them.

Designed by John P. Cheek
Cover design by Bruce Waters
Type set in Rosemary Roman/New Baskerville BT

ISBN: 978-0-7643-2798-8
Printed in China

Published by Schiffer Publishing Ltd.
4880 Lower Valley Road
Atglen, PA 19310
Phone: (610) 593-1777; Fax: (610) 593-2002
E-mail: Info@schifferbooks.com

For the largest selection of fine reference books on this and related subjects, please visit our web site at **www.schifferbooks.com**
We are always looking for people to write books on new and related subjects. If you have an idea for a book please contact us at the above address.

This book may be purchased from the publisher.
Include $3.95 for shipping.
Please try your bookstore first.
You may write for a free catalog.

In Europe, Schiffer books are distributed by
Bushwood Books
6 Marksbury Ave.
Kew Gardens
Surrey TW9 4JF England
Phone: 44 (0) 20 8392-8585; Fax: 44 (0) 20 8392-9876
E-mail: info@bushwoodbooks.co.uk
Website: www.bushwoodbooks.co.uk
Free postage in the U.K., Europe; air mail at cost.

Contents

Introduction

Portland, Oregon was born along the banks of the Willamette River, a tributary of the Columbia, the river that brought Lewis and Clark and their Corp of Discovery from a fledgling United States deep into unexplored and unknown territories. The Willamette spawned ports and the ports spawned a town. The town grew to a city populated with settlers, explorers, and adventurers — pilgrims who pushed westward as far as the continent would allow, coming to make homes here, fresh starts, or last stands.

Shipping fed Portland with traffic from all over the west coast, vessels from Washington and California, and from across the Pacific, the ships laden with trade goods, their holds heavy with the mysteries and wonders of the Far East. Innumerable cultures converged on this port town and spread out across the ancient land. American, European, Chinese, Japanese and more came to the territory once inhabited by peoples with names like the Ahantchuyuk and the Yaquina, the Nez Perce, to land once called home by tribes with no names, tribes before names, before language itself.

The weather here is dark, raining more days than not; the sky gray and heavy with thick clouds, and something about the persistence of the condition casts a melancholy pall over the green hills and scenic landscapes of the river valley. Spring is beautiful in Portland, bright with flowers and life; summer is temperate. But when the winds of fall rush through the Columbia River Gorge, when the rain returns and the days grow short, you can feel the age of the place, the history of it. You can feel the countless generations who have called this verdant, hilly land their own. Thousands on thousands of lives lived and lost. And you can feel that not all who rest here rest in peace.

There are a dozen different names for ghosts, a dozen different designations that all say almost the same thing, have almost the same meaning, but are also slightly different, nuanced: a presence versus an essence versus a manifestation versus a ghost. Before I started this book, I didn't know the difference between the words paranormal and supernatural. To a certain extent, they both mean the same thing; they mean something "beyond the range of every day human experience" or scientific explanation—as if the scientific explanation and human experience are mutually exclusive. But supernatural means more than just that and here is where the two definitions diverge: something supernatural is also above and beyond nature regardless of human experience and therefore immeasurable by the scientific constructs we have invented to explain and catalogue the things we think and see and feel.

When we move beyond the realm of science, we venture into the territory of faith. Faith is immeasurable, unquantifiable and unquestionable. We believe because we believe and that belief is what's most important about the process, not what or why, but how and, maybe more importantly, how *much*.

I gathered these tales through a number of sources: one-on-one conversations, newspaper accounts published in the *Oregonian* and the now-defunct *Oregon Journal*, I placed an ad on-line, which led to emails and more formal interviews, and I listened when someone wanted to huddle around the candle at the end of a bar and whisper a story that usually ended with someone pointing to the goose bumps on their arm and saying, "This always happens when I hear that one." I'm not sure I can say I believe every story in this book, but I believe the people who told them believe and that is why I have reported their narratives, whenever possible, in their own words. A number of individuals I interviewed were willing, and even excited, to have their story attributed to their own names in these pages, whereas others requested anonymity for a variety of personal reasons. In those cases, I have assigned fictional names where necessary or simply left the narrator unnamed.

I am indebted to everyone who took the time to talk with me and share their encounters and to everyone who listened and read while I worked on this book. The experience of investigating the paranormal in this city has made one thing clear—Portland knows its ghosts.

From the disembodied screams of a murdered girl heard beneath the gothic arches of the St. John's Bridge to the moving furniture, cold spots, and ethereal figures spotted in the popular bar and live music venue the White Eagle, Portland knows its ghosts.

From the ghostly veteran of the First World War still waiting to return home from battle to the spectral beast roaming the woods at the edge of town, Portland knows its ghost.

From the tragedy of the Shanghai Tunnels twisting beneath the waterfront, where unsuspecting men were drugged and kidnapped only to wake up on ships bound for foreign shores and women were imprisoned and forced into immoral servitude, the sounds of their grief endlessly echoing through the labyrinth, to the haunted houses, apartments, restaurants and hotels that dot the city, Portland knows its ghosts.

And, now you can know them, too.

The ancient land where Portland now stands has seen thousands of generations; even before Lewis and Clark, countless lives lived and lost. And not all who rest here rest in peace.

The Meier and Frank Building

The Meier and Frank Building stands, as it has for almost a century, as an impressive and imposing sentinel over downtown Portland. A monument to the success and prosperity of the Meier and Frank department store chain, the fifteen-story structure with a glazed terra cotta facade, was the grand vision of chain co-founder Sigmund Frank. Originally planned as an annex to the existing Meier and Frank store built in 1898, after a trip to the Midwest with Portland architect A.E. Doyle to inspect the headquarter buildings of the powerhouse retailers in Chicago, Frank conceived of a fully modern, full service retail environment that would occupy an entire city block, from Southwest Fifth Avenue and Alder Street to Southwest Sixth Avenue and Morrison Street. Tragically, Sigmund Frank never lived to see the realization of his dream. His death in 1910 resulted in the phased development of the current building, which was not completed until 1932.

Who knows how many ghosts haunt the halls of this historic structure? Scores of stories have been told over the past century encompassing everything from the spirit of an exhausted shopper who dropped

The Meier and Frank Building on the corner of Southwest 5th Avenue and Morrison Street. What restless spirits will be awakened by the current construction?

dead on the steps of the building, her arms full of packages, doomed to eternally browse the aisles in search of one last bargain, to accounts of the ghost of Sigmund Frank himself, in death enjoying the grandeur of the building fate prevented him from ever seeing completed.

Kay Hale was an employee of the Meier and Frank Corporation for most of her professional career. Starting as a clerk on the sales floor, she worked her way up the ladder until, in her own words, she became "well placed in regional management." She saw the building through several renovations and witnessed many of the historic interior elements vanish in the name of modernization. During her tenure, two areas of the store to escape destruction were the elegant Georgian Room Restaurant on the tenth floor and Santa Land, a whimsical environment providing yuletide joy to the children of Oregon and Washington for over fifty years. With its holiday model railroad display and its kid-sized monorail giving children exciting rides around the ceiling, Santa Land was in itself a Portland landmark, and was known as the home of the most authentic and enthusiastic Saint Nick in all of the Northwest.

Once Kay reached a position of responsibility, her job often required her to work late into the night. Her office was on one of the upper floors, an area dedicated primarily to the storage of old merchandise, a time capsule mausoleum entombing the remains of a century's worth of consumer culture, watched over by bald and armless mannequins half-dressed in the fashion of bygone days. On one occasion, she worked so late into the night that when she emerged from her office, she found the floor abandoned by her coworkers and all the lights off.

Not wanting to be locked in by security, she made her way through the silent floor to a dimly lit stairwell veined with the remnants of the pneumatic tube system that once ferried money and messages through the building and down to the first level. She moved through the empty building trying to find a way out, her passage illuminated only by the weak orange glow of the exit signs. Signs marking exits that were all locked. Instead of setting off an alarm, she decided to spend the night on the couch in her office.

It had been a long day and she feel asleep quickly, only to be awoken hours later by strange sounds coming from the floor outside her office door.

First, she heard the service elevator rumble to life. The metal gate slid open and slammed closed, then the car began its noisy descent to the first floor. When it stopped, she again heard the gate open and close, the sound echoing up the empty shaft, and the car started its way back up, passing Kay's floor and continuing all the way to the fifteenth floor. Again she heard the gate, then the car dropped back down to the first level. The gate again, and the car once more began its journey. Up and down it went, never pausing at any floor except the first and fifteenth.

Over the clamor of the elevator, she also heard something else, something right outside her office door—movement. Something was moving out there, sliding across the floor, scuffing and scraping as it went. And whispering. First one voice, then another, then another until it sounded like a dozen or more, speaking quietly, hushed and harsh, sometimes talking, sometimes laughing. Then she heard the crash of what sounded like boxes being thrown around, the abandoned merchandise shifting inside the containers as they were lifted and dropped to the floor. Then, as abruptly as it began, everything fell silent.

Kay was a rational woman—her rational, logical mind was the main reason she'd been so successful in business and it was what she relied on to get her through the most difficult professional and personal trials. There was a rational explanation for what she had just heard, there had to be. And it was this: the night crew had come back in the building to finish some work. They were moving some of the old merchandise to the warehouse, she'd heard the staff talking about it earlier in the week, and they had returned tonight to get a jump on the job. That was it.

Satisfied with her rationalization, Kay rose quietly from the couch, tiptoed to her office door, and locked it. She returned to the couch and was back to sleep in no time.

When she emerged from her office the next morning, a little wrinkled and only slightly embarrassed at wearing the same clothes she'd worn the day before, she approached the head of security to ask what time the stocking crew had come back to the store the night before and if it was unusual for them to return to work so late at night.

She was told no one could have been in the building. No one entered the building after the security guard had locked up for the night, the lock logs would have recorded it. Kay had passed the night in the building alone. When she protested, insisting to the guard that she'd heard the elevator and movement and voices, she was told: "It must have been the ghosts."

If anyone was familiar with the ghosts that haunt the Meier and Frank building, it was the security staff. It was one of the first "unofficial" pieces of information delivered during a new officer's orientation. If they worked in the building for any length of time, chances were they would either receive a report of an incident that could only be explained by the presence of paranormal activity or witness an event themselves.

Take the example of the Shoe Department Incident. Several mornings when the clerks staffing the shoe department came to work, they found shoes from the display racks either rearranged so lefts were with lefts and rights were with rights, pumps were with flats, loafers mated to sneakers, or that the entire display had been dumped on the floor. It's said that this happened so many times, the shoe department manager persuaded security to train a camera on the racks to record the identity of the mischievous vandal. The next time the shoe clerks came in to work to find their department in disarray, the previous night's videotape was reviewed. They fast-forwarded through hours of nothing, just a bunch of shoes sitting on the shelves, no intruder moving through the frame, no sign of supernatural activity. Until the first shoe "flew off the rack." They rewound the tape and watched it again. A single shoe, with no perceptible force acting on it, dove off the rack, as if it had come to life and leapt for freedom. The department manager and security chief stared in disbelief. They were about to rewind the tape again when they saw the next shoe hurled from the rack. It flew through the department and tumbled under a sock display. Then shoes started popping up one after another, like a flock of frightened birds suddenly taking flight and raining down across the entire department.

When asked, my contact for this story was unable to produce the tape. Surveillance tapes are routinely reused and taped over, only being archived when evidence needs to be preserved for litigation. Perhaps it's just as well. It's difficult to imagine in what court of law one would prosecute an invisible shoe-abusing apparition, anyway.

One final account of a ghostly encounter from the Meier and Frank Building is perhaps most disturbing owing to the reluctance of those involved to discuss the incident. This narrative originated with former members of the night cleaning crew, but the reports of the story, though there are several, are all second-hand.

One morning, as soon as the day staff arrived for work, they received a message from every member of the night cleaning crew: they were quitting, effective immediately. They did not elaborate beyond declaring they would "never spend another night in that building."

Eventually, rumors began to drift back to the management staff. The cleaning crew had been working on the tenth floor near the end of their shift when they cut through the kitchen of the Georgian Room. What they saw there drove them off the floor and out of the building, never to return, not even to pick up their final paychecks. Some report that, like the shoes on the retail floor, objects in the kitchen began flying off the counters, rocketing to every corner of the room, smashing against the walls and powdering the kitchen with spices and flour and broken glass. Still others have made vague allusions to a "presence" the crew encountered, something hostile and threatening... something that chased the crew out of the kitchen. And others have said that whatever was seen there was "too terrible to describe." Whatever it was, it was real enough, and disturbing enough to convince a half dozen people to leave their jobs without a second thought. Or so the story goes.

Whatever the haunted history of the Meier and Frank Building is, that history is drawing to a close. In 1967, St. Louis-based Mays Department Store purchased the Meier and Frank chain. The store maintained the Meier and Frank name and branding after the acquisition, but after Mays merged with Federated, the parent company of Macy's, the Meier and Frank name and the building itself began its journey into obsolescence. Most of the historic building has been earmarked for conversion into a 330-room luxury hotel. As of this writing, construction has already begun. The Georgian Room has been slated for demolition and Santa Land will be disassembled, moved, and reassembled in another location. The monorail will no longer provide rides to children, but will be retained as a nonfunctioning display, a backdrop for holiday photographs. It's uncertain what the construction crews may discover as they continue with the renovations, or whom they may disturb. Whether it's the spectral energy of excited children, primed for play and mischief by the excitement of an eternal Christmas, or the spirit of Sigmund Frank, perhaps distressed to see the enterprise he co-founded consumed by a massive retail conglomerate, one thing is certain: the Meier and Frank Building *is* haunted, at least by the collective memories of those who recall a Portland that is steadily fading into the past, if not by more.

Ghost Dog

A young woman in her senior year at Reed College rented a small, one-bedroom trailer on an isolated, wooded piece of property in far-east Portland. She moved there in search of a little solitude; after six semesters of crowded dorms and too many roommates in tiny apartments, she was looking forward to some privacy. She lived in the trailer comfortably for a week before she noticed anything unusual. The first night of her second week, just as she was climbing into her narrow bed, she heard the distant, plaintive howls of what sounded like a large, injured dog. The wailing lasted all night and into the early hours of morning. Before leaving for class the next day, she walked down the long dirt driveway expecting to find some sign of the animal in the road. But there was nothing.

The next night she was washing her dinner dishes in the sink, gazing out the window and thinking about the homework she had to do before bed. Her trailer was almost a hundred yards from the road and at night the only sign of civilization visible through her kitchenette window was a lone streetlight. Any illumination it provided was spent entirely on the road. After sunset, with thick winter clouds obscuring the

19

pallid glow of the moon, her tiny trailer was adrift in a sea of darkness.

That's when she caught her first glimpse of it.

Out there, under the streetlight, faraway, something flashed across the road. It was large but difficult to see, fast and she only glimpsed it for a second. She leaned closer to the thin glass of the window, straining to see. Had it been a dog? *The* dog? She held her breath to keep from fogging the glass.

Then, the terrible howls erupted in the night, rolling across the empty lot and rattling the windows of the trailer. The animal sounded closer than the night before. Closer and more frantic.

She tripped over her feet backing out of the small kitchen. She hit the floor hard and for a moment she considered staying there, pressing her hands over her ears and waiting for the terrible sound to stop. But looking up into the trailer she knew she had to move. The trailer got so hot when she used the oven, even with a fan, she'd gotten in the habit of leaving the front door open.

The first night she heard the creature, she'd taken it to be an injured dog, maybe hit by a car or attacked by something wild. Even though she was technically inside the city limits, this area felt like the country to her. When she was alone in her cramped home and her imagination went to work, she could picture all kinds of feral animals roaming through the trees. She even felt a little guilty for not going out to investigate. But now, she knew she'd been wrong. No earthly animal could make that kind of noise, nothing that lived and breathed.

On all fours, she scrambled into the living room. The storm door on the trailer opened out and the main door opened in. Both were thin and suddenly seemed a lot less substantial than when she first moved in. Reaching out into the night, she grabbed the storm door and pulled it closed. She latched it, glancing out toward the street, desperately searching for any sign of the beast. Then she slammed the front door, locked it, and shot home the deadbolt.

The mad howls of the creature seemed to crescendo then, a dozen desperate voices woven into a whirlwind of suffering, yowling shrieks and growls that simultaneously terrified and filled her with an unbearable sense of sadness.

Then – silence.

She waited, expecting the other worldly cacophony to start up again, but for the rest of the evening, the only sound she heard was the beating of her own panicked heart.

The next morning, as soon as the sun rose, she threw a shopping bag full of clothes in her truck and drove off to stay with friends in town.

After a week of couch hopping, the memories of that night in the trailer started to fade. Maybe it *was* only a hurt dog or something. Maybe she'd let her imagination run away with her. After all, it *was* kind of creepy out there all alone. Maybe she'd just worked herself up into a state of panic and over-reacted to something easily explainable. Besides, she quickly got tired of camping in her friends' living room and she suspected they were getting a little tired of her squatting there. So after a week, she drove back to the property, hoping that the dinner dishes she'd left in the sink hadn't become too funky and telling herself there was nothing to be afraid of, nothing at all.

She turned off the main road after the streetlight and drove slowly up the long, dirt driveway. Nothing about the property was different. The trailer was exactly as she left it: dirty clothes on the floor, dishes in the sink. She spent the day cleaning and straightening, studying, and after dark, she took a long shower in the tiny bathroom and climbed into bed.

A nimbus moon cast dull light through the small windows of the trailer. Listening to the night silence, she told herself there was nothing out there, nothing out there, nothing out there, until she started to drift off to sleep.

A sound woke her in the small hours of the morning, a weak *scratch, scratch, scratch* at the front door. Then a whine, a high pitched, pleading sound. Then *scratch, scratch, scratch.*

She jumped from her bed just as something enormous smashed into the door. The entire trailer rocked as the door was pawed and battered, the thin whine growing into the intolerable howls of the ghost dog.

She screamed and threw herself back on the bed, her voice was all but lost in the din of the beast. There was no place to hide in the trailer; the bathroom was separated from the main area only by a plastic, accordion door. It didn't even latch. The bedroom only had a curtain. If it got in, there was no place to hide.

She pressed herself into the corner as far away from the door as she could. The pounding continued, it wanted in, whatever it was, it wanted in desperately.

And then, it got what it wanted.

It didn't crash the door open, it didn't force the metal to buckle and break, but it got in. Through half-closed eyes she saw it pass *through* the door. If it had been a dog, that was long ago. What passed through the door and leapt into the trailer was something else now; something twisted and pained, the color of mist, the consistency of smoke. It flowed into the trailer and flew straight toward her bed. She threw the covers over her face and she felt it, cold and heavy, collide with her and begin to dig frantically at her through the blanket. It whined, it cried, it howled and growled.

And then... it was gone.

This time she didn't wait until morning, she didn't take the time to grab any clothes. She ran as fast as she could to her truck and sped away from the trailer, sure the whole time it was behind her, chasing her down the lonely road.

She drove through the night until she reached her parent's house in upstate Washington. She didn't tell them why she'd come, she just asked if she could stay for awhile. The next morning, she called the old woman she'd rented the trailer from and told her she was out, after she collected her things, she was never going back to the trailer and she could charge her a re-renting fee and keep her deposit if she wanted, but she was never going back.

The old woman didn't sound surprised—this wasn't the first time. That trailer was so hard to rent, and the old woman explained that ten years before, a woman had lived there with her dog. One night, the tenant connected a hose to her car exhaust, ran the hose through the kitchen window, and started the engine. Her dog had been tied up outside, but somehow the animal had known something was wrong. It chewed through its leash and forced its way into the trailer. But by then it was too late, the small trailer was too full of deadly carbon monoxide. When they found them, it looked like the dog had tried to revive its owner by scratching her and biting her, but to no avail. Eventually the dog, too, was overcome. Its body was discovered on the bed next to its master, loyal and protective through life, into death and, apparently, beyond.

Edgefield

A man and woman reserved a room at Edgefield, the 38-acre McMenamin's hotel and estate at the mouth of the Columbia River Gorge, to celebrate their anniversary. They made the short drive to the hotel together late in the afternoon and, as soon as they checked in and dropped off their bags in the room, went down to the restaurant for an early dinner. As they ate, the man became extraordinarily fatigued, as if he'd been up for days. He could barely keep his eyes open during the meal. He excused himself and went back to the room to lie down while his wife finished eating.

The building that houses the main hotel on the Edgefield Estate dates back to 1911. The whole European-style village is made up of richly restored buildings, some of which were once home to a facility known as the Multnomah County Poor Farm. The room the couple was staying in had been a part of the infirmary and at one time, the orphanage. As the man headed toward the room, he became even more tired, as if something was draining his energy with each step. Without undressing, he dropped down on the bed and fell instantly to sleep. But his rest was not a peaceful one. He was assaulted with disturbing dreams, dreams of unbearable hunger

and depravation, fear and pain, and a desperate lone-
liness that made him sob in his sleep. He remained in
this unbearable state until his wife returned to the room
and, after much effort, managed to wake him.

He tried to explain to his wife what he'd just
experienced, but found it almost impossible to describe. The feelings had been so visceral, so real and
overwhelming that he could scarcely find the words
to express them.

His wife tried to rouse and reassure him. They had
many plans for the evening, a walk around the garden
and a movie at the theater. It was their anniversary,
after all, and they'd been looking forward to the trip
for weeks. Her husband complained of extreme thirst
and she brought him a glass of water before stepping
into the bathroom to freshen up. There, she was seized
by the same oppressive tiredness. Her energy instantly
drained from her body and she almost fainted. As she
fought to hold onto her balance, something unseen
slammed into her, a rough shove that nearly knocked
her off her feet. It yanked on her hair and pawed at her
face. She screamed for her husband and ran back into
the room only to find him again unconscious on the
bed. This time, he wouldn't wake up and only moaned
in his sleep before rolling away from her. She shook
him and yelled his name, but as she did, she felt herself
begin to slip into oblivion and sink down on the bed
next to him. She was nearly out herself when, in a last
ditch effort to save both of them, she grabbed the glass
of water from the nightstand and threw it in his face.

That did the trick. With her help, her husband
struggled to pull himself from the bed and drag his

wife up after him. Without a word, they both grabbed their still-packed bags and ran for the car.

The energy-draining exhaustion and oppressive presence clung to them like a fog as they sped away from the hotel. They thought they would feel better as they got further away, but they didn't, and the man had to fight to keep control on the winding road. After a hairpin turn forced them to slow down the couple caught sight of something in their rearview mirror and realized they were being pursued.

They could see it in the red glow of their taillights, close enough to cut through the pluming clouds of exhaust. It looked like a naked child, or what had once been a child, but now its features were distorted and hideous. Its head was hairless and swollen, grotesquely encephalitic and lolling at the end of a long, thin neck. Its mouth was drawn down and twisted into a mournful "O" and a horrible wail issued from it and shrieked through the cold night. Its arms where ghastly and elongated past reason, dragging along the ground and flapping behind, as it pursued the car with its loping, uneven gait. They were going better than sixty miles an hour but the apparition had no trouble keeping up, its misshapen feet barely making contact with the pavement as it raced after them.

In the rearview mirror, the man saw the wraith lift those awful, impossible arms and strain to reach them, its expression plaintive and pained, imploring.

Finally, the road straightened out and the man was able to stomp down on the accelerator. Unfortunately, their car was badly in need of a tune up. As a matter of fact, he'd promised to get that done as a part of his anniversary present – just as soon as they got home from their trip. The moment he gunned it, the engine choked and threatened to stall. The creature gained ground then and its terrible arms reached within an inch of their bumper. The couple broke out in shouts of frustration and fear, but finally the engine revved and the car lurched forward, the speedometer edging past seventy-five and heading north of eighty as they flew down the road.

The specter chasing them waved its insane arms in frustration and the sound that escaped it was both horrible and heart-wrenching, like a chorus of frightened children. Eventually, the couple out-paced the phantom and they sped toward home with a combination of relief, horror, and terrible sadness.

This is the first story I heard about Edgefield, before I heard about the impressive hotel, about the brew pubs and the movie theater, before I went out there and saw those fantastic old buildings and the spectacular scenery of the Columbia River Gorge on the drive. McMenamins has made something really special in Troutdale, and whereas I didn't personally experience anything supernatural during my stay, I heard plenty of stories, not all as disturbing as this one, many recorded in the guest's "ghost log" kept for visitors who might want to document any spectral encounters. And I had a great time doing it. There were tales of ghost lights and a phantom flute that plays late at night. There have even been reports of playful spirits that tickle feet and ruffle hair. And as long as Edgefield's doors are open to ghost hunters and fun-loving guests, I'm sure there will be more.

Crow Bar

They call him Private Paul, though nobody really knows his rank or name. He's a soldier on his way home from the war, still in uniform, and still bearing the emotional and physical scars of combat, tormented by his experience. But the war ended long ago and Private Paul has been waiting for his final journey home for over ninety years.

Crow Bar on North Mississippi Street opened on New Year's Eve 2003 in a long, narrow building that juts off a larger stone and brick structure, now broken up into apartments that once served as a halfway facility for soldiers returning from World War I. It is in those rooms, as well as the bar below, that Private Paul waits for his injuries to heal and his discharge papers to arrive.

Patrick, one of the owners of Crow Bar, tells of Private Paul's activity. On one occasion, he and the bartender were closing up when several bottles of liquor were shoved off their shelves. It wasn't every bottle in a row, but random bottles deliberately knocked over one at a time and dropping down to open the beer taps below. Marie, a current employee, went down to the basement one night for ice. On her way to the freezer, she found a chair blocking her path. She

The spirit of "Private Paul", a World War I veteran who never made it home from the war, haunts Crow Bar on North Mississippi Street. *Photo courtesy Joshua Wilson.*

moved the chair, pushing it over to the wall, but when she emerged from the freezer with the ice, the chair had been moved back. She moved it again and hurried back to the bar, certain she heard the sounds of footsteps and labored breathing in the empty basement behind her. Customers have reported candles sliding slowly across the bar and that prickly feeling you get on the back of your neck when someone is standing right behind you. Of course, when they turn to investigate, there's never anyone there. Private Paul seems a little mischievous when he's in the bar. Soldiers like to have a good time when they're off duty and maybe that's what he's doing, cutting loose a little, but up in the apartments above the bar, Private Paul's mood darkens. One area psychic who has investigated the site feels that Private Paul spent his last days in one of the rooms of the rehabilitation facility, waiting to recover from his injuries enough to finish the journey home. A journey he was never able to take.

A young woman named Jen lived in one of the apartments above the bar and it is from her that we have the most detailed description of Private Paul. Jen and a friend were watching television in her living room late one night with the lights off and only a couple of candles placed around the room for illumination. All at once, as if a strong wind had blown through the apartment, the candles were snuffed out. In darkness broken only by the dim flicker of her black and white television, they heard a familiar creaking sound begin and the disturbing wheezing of someone battling to catch each breath. Jen's friend tried to relight the candles, but the wicks wouldn't take, they would just hiss and go out. When they turned on the overhead light, they saw Paul.

"He was there in the rocking chair my grandmother gave me," Jen said. "Barely there, but I could make out his outline. At first I thought he was some kind of cowboy because he had this wide brimmed hat on, but when I looked closer, I could see he was in a military uniform with high leather boots and an empty holster at his side." Jen and her friend didn't know what to do. They watched the Private, rocking back and forth and staring out the window, battling to take each breath, until the specter let out one final sigh and disappeared. "It scared us, a lot, but something about seeing him was also really sad."

The Private's symptoms seem consistent with a number of veterans whose lungs were burned by mustard gas and clogged with scar tissue, the labored breathing and the slow, painful decline as they suffocated, sometimes over the course of months. Is that what happened to Private Paul? Did he manage to survive through combat only to come back to the states and slowly strangle while waiting to go home? According to the psychic, it's not just possible, it's likely. "Imagine the disappointment," he told me, "imagine the frustration of living through the slaughter of St. Mihiel or the second battle of the Somme, only to make it back to the states and die in a strange place still so far from home. It's heartbreaking."

It is heartbreaking. As heartbreaking as the realization that, where as the war to end all wars may have ended almost one hundred years ago, for Private Paul in the building on North Mississippi, the wait for peace goes on.

"I won't let them hurt you"

Kelly is twenty-seven years old. She moved to Portland after graduating from Iowa State with a degree
in design. She's about 5'3" or 4" with long, curly black
hair, a pale complexion, and very clear, very blue eyes.
She didn't smile a lot while we talked, but when she
did it was bright and wide and infectious. We met
one afternoon at the Rogue Brewery on the corner
of Northwest 13th Avenue and Flanders Street. The
weather was turning nice so we sat outside. She was
quiet and polite and sat anxiously twisting her hands
in her lap while the waitress took our order. When
we were alone, she leaned in close and whispered, "I
hope you know I'm not crazy."

Kelly had answered the on-line ad I placed looking for ghost stories. Her email was short and without
detail. It said simply, "I have something I have to
tell you," she wrote. "Something I have to tell someone."

She barely waited for me to get my tape recorder
out before she started talking.

"When I moved to Portland, I moved in with a
friend from college. She was from here and we got an
apartment together in north Portland in the Kenton

area ... a big stone building. It wasn't really a nice place, but it was ours and it was my first place on my own, and when we moved in, we spent a lot of time fixing it up and listening to music and having a good time."

Kelly said the neighborhood wasn't bad during the day; the area was fairly diverse with everything from college students to retirees living there. She always felt safe during the day, but at night "... it got a little sketchy. There were some homeless people who always hung out around the corner and there was this nasty bar down the street." When the bar closed at two in the morning, raucous patrons would pour into the street drunk and scream at each other. "It was scary."

After Kelly had lived in the apartment for about a month, her roommate got a new boyfriend and started staying at his place most nights. "I didn't care at first, I was kind of glad, we weren't getting along like we did in college and I was happy to have the place to myself. But I got a little nervous at night."

She told me about a fight she had with her roommate. Kelly wasn't just a designer, but also an artist, and she'd hung a number of her favorite prints in the hallway between the bedrooms. Her roommate's boyfriend was also an artist and when they started dating, he gave her a large painting he'd done as a school project. Kelly hated it and there was no way they were going to hang it in the living room. Her roommate didn't want to put it in her bedroom because she said that would be rude. It was great art, she said, and they should display it. The only other place to put it was the hallway where Kelly had her prints.

But Kelly resisted and they fought over it. Her art was art, too, and it meant a whole lot more to her than the amateurish Pollock pastiches of her roommate's loser boyfriend.

"But after a while, I just got tired of it being a thing. So one night, I was lying in bed and decided to do something about it right then. I got up and took all my prints off the wall. I took them down and just left them in a corner. I wasn't going to hang *his* painting, but I figured I'd make the gesture and the next time she came back to the apartment, she'd see and we could quit talking about it."

Kelly went back to bed, feeling better because she'd done the mature thing, and finally managed to drift off to sleep.

"The next morning, I felt good, you know? I felt like I'd done the grown up thing and we could move on." Her roommate wasn't home yet when she got up and Kelly even thought about leaving her a note saying she was sorry they had fought. But when she came out of her room that morning, "All my pictures were back on the wall."

She thought that maybe she'd dreamed taking them down, that it was something she'd been thinking about doing while going to sleep and something she'd *meant* to do, but hadn't actually done. She took the prints down again and put them back in the corner, then put the whole thing out of her mind.

For several weeks, nothing else out of the ordinary occurred. Kelly started a job for a web-based training company and became indoctrinated into the sched-ule demands of an agency career while her roommate started spending more and more time at her boyfriend's. Kelly would usually get home after eight, find the apartment empty, fix some dinner, watch a little TV, and then collapse into bed.

"The first time I heard him, I thought I was losing my mind."

Despite the fact that Kelly had come to appreciate her roommate's absence, the neighborhood had taken a definite turn for the worse. Her bedroom was on the first floor and faced the street. One night she heard a fight that she later saw on the news ended in a stabbing. Twice she awoke to the sound of gunshots. And once, in the middle of the night, she woke to see a face pressed against her window, trying to see in.

"I was starting to have trouble sleeping. Work was harder than I expected and I was stressed out about that. I came from a big family and I'm used to a house full of people. Even in college, I lived in the dorm and there were always people around. Living in that apartment, in that neighborhood, it was different. I started to be scared all the time."

She'd become accustomed to hearing voices right outside her window, after awhile that wouldn't even wake her up anymore. What she wasn't used to was hearing voices *in* the apartment.

One night Kelly was in bed, late, she said it had to be after 2 or 3 a.m. The street had quieted down and she felt like she was finally going to get some rest when the murmuring started. "At first it sounded like it was coming from the hall, right next to the painting." She thought maybe it was her roommate, or maybe her roommate's boyfriend, that they'd come in late to crash and were talking quietly so they wouldn't wake her up.

"But it wasn't two voices, it was only one."

She could never tell what it was saying, but she was sure it was the same voice all the time, a man's voice, low and mumbling, constant, like "someone having a conversation with themselves."

The next morning, the boyfriend's painting was on the floor, crushed on one end, like it had been stepped on.

Kelly figured they'd just hung it poorly; it was pretty big and heavy and the one nail hammered into the sheetrock couldn't have been enough to hold it up. "But why didn't I hear it fall in the night?"

"I asked my roommate if she'd come home that night. She thought I was talking about the painting and she wanted to fight about it because she thought I knocked it down. But I was talking about the voice I heard."

But her roommate hadn't been in the apartment, neither had her boyfriend. Kelly had been alone that night.

That was about it for the shared living experience *and* the apartment. Her roommate announced she was moving in with her boyfriend immediately and Kelly knew she couldn't afford the two-bedroom on her own. She'd have to find her own place in the next three weeks and put together the money to cover all the moving expenses.

That stressed her out even more and if she'd had trouble sleeping before, it was nothing compared to what the next three weeks would bring.

Kelly was exhausted all the time, dragging herself out of bed in the morning, stumbling through the workday, then meeting with landlords and property managers while she tried to find an affordable place to live.

One night, just as she felt like she was about to drift off, a fight erupted outside her window. There were shouts and curses and the flat crack of fists impacting flesh.

"It really scared me," she said. "I just got really emotional and started to freak out and cry and yell that I was calling the police and I had a gun." She closed her eyes and covered her face with the blankets.

And then she heard the voice.

It started out in the hall, right outside her door, the same low mumbling. Then it moved into her room, past her bed, across the floor and stopped by the window.

Kelly held her breath and listened. She still couldn't make out what he was saying, but the voice was constant. She listened carefully to the stream of speech, trying to pick out words, like someone straining to hear a distant radio signal on a poorly tuned receiver. She finally made out one sentence, one sentence repeated over and over through the stream of nonsense. She heard the voice say, "I won't let them hurt you."

Kelly lowered the blankets from her face and opened her eyes.

"He was standing by the window, looking out toward the street."

She said she saw the vague shape of a tall man, only

partially distinct in the half-light of the street lamp glowing through her curtains. He was dressed in worn jeans and work boots and stood there by her window watching the fight as still as a statue or a sentry manning his post, the low, slow speech droning into the night. She watched him for several minutes until her room erupted in the flash bulb pops of red and blue announcing the arrival of a City of Portland patrol car rolling up on the scene.

"Then I couldn't see him any more, but I *know* he'd been there. And I could still hear him, the whole time the cops were out there breaking up the fight and arresting the guys." Then, as the patrol car pulled away and the night grew quiet, his voice faded and Kelly was alone.

"But I wasn't afraid any more."

Eventually, she slept.

Two days later, Kelly moved out. Her new apartment was a lot smaller and cost a little more than her half of the rent on the old place, but with the help of her friends from work, she moved gladly into the sunny studio near Southeast Belmont and resolved to put the whole three month experience behind her.

It wasn't until moving day that Kelly asked one of her neighbors about who had lived in the apartment before her. The long-time resident told her the unit had been vacant for some time, he wasn't sure why, but the manager had a hard time filling it. "Maybe it's all the noise from the street." Before that, a man named Timber and his mother had occupied it.

"Timber?" Kelly asked, "Like what you say when a tree falls?"

The neighbor told her that was right. His name
was Tim, but everyone called him Timber because
he was so tall and so straight and would stand there
sometimes just as still as a tree. "He was a little different," the neighbor told her, "a little slow." But he was
a good guy and he and his mother took care of each
other until she died. After she died, the neighbor figured, Timber must have gotten lonely and he started
drinking at the bar down the street to find company.
Timber needed to have someone to take care of just
as much he needed someone to look out for him. The
neighbor wasn't sure what happened to Timber, but
he had heard that after Timber started hanging out
with the bar crowd, he'd come to "no good end."

Kelly moved out and moved on, but she's never
gotten over the feeling of having someone near her
at times of stress. She knew it had been Timber in her
room that night, that it had been Timber who put her
prints back on the wall after she'd taken them down.
He'd been looking out for her, being a good guy, and
taking care of her at a time in her life when she'd
never felt more alone.

"A House too Haunted"

How does the mind work after death, if it works at all? What are they thinking, the spirits and wraiths, those returned and those who never really left? It's difficult to imagine what anyone would think, or how, after the trauma of death. Do spirits carry the psychic scars of the people they once were? And if they do, does that help explain why they come here and why they stay when so many of the departed move past this common world and into something infinitely more mysterious?

It's generally held that ghosts return for a half dozen or so recurring reasons. They return seeking proper burial, they return frequently to a place they loved or hated, to a place where they felt great joy or great sorrow. They can come to guard and protect loved ones, or they can come seeking vengeance or to create havoc.

But what happens when more than one entity returns to inhabit the same territory, when there is more than one haunting in a single location, where the spirits meet in conflict, attempting to occupy the same piece of corporeal real estate?

Sharon Nolan was a 33-year-old single mother and medical billing specialist who lived in Beaverton, Oregon in the house that had belonged to her mother. She lived with her 4-year-old daughter Lily and her widowed step-father, Graham, and despite the tragic loss of the family's matriarch just over a year before, they lived happily together with a pleasant normalcy that belied the preternatural events that were about to take place.

Sharon noticed the disturbances first in her bedroom. Her bedroom was at the front of the house next to her daughter's. It was large and bright, comfortable, and a place where she'd always been relaxed and happy. But lately, she'd begun to feel uneasy when she was there alone, nervous, like someone was watching her, someone she couldn't see. At the same time, she found herself thinking of her mother more. Not so uncommon, it hadn't been long since she lost her mom, but she found herself thinking about her in a way she hadn't since her mother first died. Not with the distant sense of memory, but with a feeling of immediacy, proximity. She felt her mother close.

Sharon did her best to ignore the odd feelings, put them out of her mind and go about her business, but when her daughter Lily started waking up in the middle of the night, every night, complaining about bad dreams and more, Sharon had to admit that something strange was happening in the house. Lily said there was something in her closet, something trying to get into the house. She told her mother, "But Grandma won't let them."

Sharon met Angela Renee through coworkers and the two soon became friends. Angela Renee, 26-years-old, was originally from Memphis, Tennessee and is a certified Spiritual Counselor. She could tell something was bothering her friend and, as they got to know each other, Sharon confided in Angela about the strange occurences in her house.

As a Spiritual Counselor, Angela's services included readings, investigations and cleansing rituals. She wasn't sure what the problem at Sharon's house was, or where it was coming from, but she knew it was a problem and one that she urged her friend to look into as soon as possible. Sharon invited Angela to her home for dinner; as friends, just to eat and talk and hang out, but also to get a feel for the strange energy surrounding her home and to see if there was anything that could be done about it.

It was a large house on the outskirts of Beaverton, just outside of Portland, with several rooms stretching across a generous plot of land and a large addition built onto the house several years after the initial construction. The main entrance led into the dining room; off to the right were Angela and Lily's bedrooms, a bathroom and the garage. To the left there was the living room, the kitchen, and another long hallway to the back where Sharon's stepfather lived in one of the three additional bedrooms. Before dinner, Sharon asked Angela if she'd like a tour. Angela said she would, very much. She'd felt something as soon as she'd reached the property, as soon as she'd parked her car in the driveway, and waited in the driver's seat for a few minutes, trying to reconcile the conflicting sensations she'd felt sweeping over her. Angela didn't even have to walk inside, didn't even have to get out of her car, to know something wasn't right in the large house.

"There are a lot of different types of ghosts," Angela told me. "Some are attracted to a particular place or person. Some are just the negative residual energy that builds up in a specific location over time. Sometimes you get spectral energy that's kind of stuck in a time glitch going through repetitive behaviors like trying to get home or trying to contact someone. These aren't all necessarily the souls of people who've died, but they may be. They may be anything."

Angela walked with Sharon and Lily through the house. She immediately moved to the wing where their bedrooms were. The rooms weren't back to back, but separated by a long stretch of hallway. Angela hesitated there, studying the space between the two doors. Then she felt compelled to turn and look back into the living room, back toward the apex of a triangle drawn between the two doors and the center of the house. She looked back toward the living room and kitchen area, sensing something. That was when 4-year-old Lily said, "That's where I see Grandma."

Angela asked how often she saw her grandmother and Lily told her sometimes, especially when she was scared, when she woke up in the middle of the night and crept through the dark hallway to climb in bed with her mother. It was then that Sharon finally admitted to Angela there was more to the experience than she'd told her. She hadn't just been feeling her mother, thinking about her and missing her, but she had seen her on more than one occasion, usually just her familiar shape through the corner of her eye, moving busily through the living room and the kitchen, "Mom's territory," as she called it. "Watching out for us."

Angela was intrigued by the sightings of Sharon's mother, but her immediate concern was the sense she got from the area between the two bedrooms. She asked what was behind the wall and Sharon told her it was the closet that linked the two rooms. Lily told her the closet was where the bad dreams came from, the monsters and, "the shadows."

Angela decided to take a closer look.

The closet between the rooms was long and narrow. Angela entered through Lily's room and was immediately struck by a profound sense of disharmony. "The whole set up of the space was wrong," she said. The long closet, oddly placed between the two rooms, formed an energy vacuum that unbalanced the feng shui of both bedrooms, creating a kind of portal where spectral entities could bounce around in limitless directions. "Almost like a whirlpool effect, unstable energy flying through it... It's not the kind of place where you would find just one particular being or one spirit in your house. You could have anything passing through at any time: good spirit, bad spirit. Anything."

As she continued the tour of the house, Angela began to suspect this job might be too much for her to handle on her own. Not only did she feel the presence of Sharon's mother in the living room and kitchen and the myriad of wraiths just the other side of the portal, but she also sensed something else, something elusive.

Toward the back of the house, where the addition with the step-father's room and the empty bedrooms were, "The house noticeably darkened." Angela didn't know what caused it, or why, but the sensation she experienced when investigating that part of the structure felt wrong, unpleasant and threatening. The presence of Sharon's mother was a warm and comforting one, the closet between Lily and Sharon's room, albeit a little overwhelming, was not malicious. But a dark under-current of negative emotion, pain and anger, ran through the home, flowing toward the addition at the back of the house, "like a river of despair."

In spite of that, Angela decided to try a cleansing on her own, something to provide Sharon and Lily a little relief. She began the cleansing by burning sage, moving through the house, and gently asking the spirits to leave, asking the energy of the space to clean up, and any spectral agents to move on.

"I always start with asking," Angela said. She always starts with a little gentle persuasion, but she felt immediate resistance. Not just from the curious entities probing the boundaries of the closet portal, but a deeper, stubborn resolve not to relinquish control of the home. She was not welcome there, that was obvious, and she felt determined opposition to her cleansing efforts.

This job was indeed bigger than one person.

Angela decided to call in reinforcements. She left that night making a mental checklist of the problem spots in the house and trying to sort out the many conflicting entities she'd encountered. She left formulating a plan she felt had the greatest chance of success, unaware the whole time of the one very important factor she had overlooked.

She returned less than a week later, this time with two companions, Joanie and Dale, both spiritual counselors and cleansers with whom she'd worked before. She briefed them on her experience in the house, about the trouble spots she'd noted and the resistance she encountered when she tried a cleansing on her own, and the three came prepared for a difficult and draining task.

Each member of the team completed their personal preparations before driving to the house; ritual cleansing baths and smudging their energy, a traditional purification rite meant to cleanse all negative energy from the body and environment. Each wore a protective emblem representative of their individual faiths, an amulet, a crystal, and a crucifix. And they all brought with them the specialized tools of their trade: holy or blessed water and oil to act as a repellent, sage and incense as purifying agents, wards and fetishes.

Immediately upon arrival the team erected an altar in the living room. Since this was the part of the home where Sharon's mother was most dominant it would serve as a base of operations and a safety zone. Sharon and Lily elected to stay there while the three went about their business.

They approached the closet first. Though Angela had told them about her encounter there, the two newcomers were still surprised by the intensity of the many spectral entities they found and their determination to pass through the portal. Angela, Joanie, and Dale began their energy raising with chants and incantations, calling on the powers of the spiritual world to lend them strength, and began sending waves of positive energy back into the portal. Like before, they began by asking the entities to leave, to move on and vacate the space they had occupied. They stood with their arms out-stretched, asking the intruders to leave the people in peace and call off their invasion. But the more they sent the love and light, the more the entities were drawn to them.

"They were intrigued by us," Angela said, "and by the fact that we were giving them energy of any kind."

Still, they continued on, convinced this obstacle could be overcome if they worked together. It looked like it might work, too, until there was a drastic and unexpected turn of events.

"It was amazing," Angela said. "It was just this regular closet, but when I looked off into a corner I saw this big, expanding dark space." Something else was forcing its way through, something more than the benign entities they'd first encountered, something malignant and forceful, an expanse of nothingness, like a swirling cloud of thick ink in water, viscous with smoky tendrils winding out from the central mass. Dale suspected there was more to this portal than the convergence of circumstance they first diagnosed. He asked Sharon if there was an attic in the house. She told him there was – it ran directly over the two bedrooms. Dale was immediately dispatched to investigate while Angela and Joanie held their ground at the closet.

The entrance to the attic was a trapdoor-ladder in the ceiling of the garage. The attic itself was low and claustrophobic, the atmosphere sharp and stifling hot with the sting of insulation. The attic had been cleaned out recently, but toward the back, directly above the space between the two bedrooms, Dale found something. Something important. Something Angela had overlooked.

Sharon's mother had died in the house a little more than a year before, but hers wasn't the only passing that had occurred in the home. Two deaths took place in that house, cruel deaths protracted by the pitiless course of cancer. Sharon was young when her father died and her memories of him were colored by the distance of youth. He'd never been a man in her mind, only a father, an image made heroic and mythic by the passage of years. She'd always regretted never knowing him as an adult. But hidden in the attic this whole time were revealing clues to the depth of her father's humanity; the writings and journals he'd kept during the final year of his life.

Dale knew this was a powerful focal point for residual energy, maybe one of the most potent he'd ever encountered. The box of papers had been in the attic since it was placed there following the death of Sharon's father, undiscovered and undisturbed for all those years, festering in negative psychic energy. And if spectral energy attracts spectral energy, then this could be the key factor in the instability of the portal directly beneath the attic. Dale scanned the contents of the small box quickly, then wriggled out of the tight space and delivered it to Sharon.

Sharon found the journal was a place for her father to vent his frustration, fear, and despair during his illness while maintaining an outward appearance of confidence and strength for his family. All in the face of his own mortality. "It wasn't exactly welcoming the light kind of stuff," Angela said. With Sharon's consent, Dale took the box to an empty bedroom where, in seclusion, he prepared to channel the forceful emotion they all felt radiating from the collection of writings.

Back at the closet, Angela and Joanie felt an almost instant shift in the intensity of the resistance they were encountering. The persistence of the curious entities appeared to subside and the dark space began to recede.

They chanted and drew as much energy as they could and now Joanie and Angela commanded the entities to retreat and the portal to close. "As soon as they noticed our energy was willing to fight, it started to back off. Then it was like any animal, like a cat that senses danger and rears back, spitting, not happy, but going anyway." Angela admitted they never would have been able to do it on their own. She is convinced to this day they had more than their share of help, not from this world, but from the next. "Sharon's mom was with us the whole time," standing by their side, supporting them, looking after her home and family. "It's always good to have that kind of energy on your side when you're encountering other spectral beings."

Once the portal was closed, they employed their oils and finished with a blessing. Angela made the sign of the pentacle and Joanie made the sign of the cross and they placed seals of protection around both Sharon and Lily's bedrooms. Angela suggested Sharon buy Lily a dream catcher, just as a preventative measure, and maybe a protective emblem or statue to stand guard over the closet door.

Dale emerged from the back bedroom and returned the box of her father's writings to Sharon. He'd done what he could, and it had helped, but to truly ease her father's spirit, Sharon would have to confront her family's past on her own. What exactly Dale had done to begin to break the cycle of negative energy, he never said. He never spoke openly about the experience at all beyond telling the rest of the group the encounter had been "exhausting."

The closet and bedrooms were clean and sealed, the living room and dining room were clear and "felt of home and family", the grief of Sharon's father had been released and the comforting presence of Sharon's mother still lingered. But still, everything wasn't right about the house. Something held on, something they could all feel, something "ancient."

"It wasn't anyone's individual energy," Angela said, "and it wasn't a part of the entities in the closet or anything directly related to the house."

With so many psychic events taking place in the house, the team had all but missed the disturbing presence. Angela had noted before that the back of the house "darkened", but with the distraction of all the other activity, she'd underestimated its importance. "It wasn't the house as much as it was the land where the addition had been built. There was something about it different from the rest of the property."

The team fanned out across the lot to investigate. When Angela came around to the back of the house, she found that "even walking around that part, it felt different, even from the other ground. It felt soft and pliant: hilly." As if the ground had been churned, dug up and reburied in hills and small mounds. "I suppose it could have been a landfill once," Angela said. "That, or something else."

They discussed attempting a cleansing of the land itself, but such a massive space required more strength than the three could muster. "We went out and looked around, but there was just too much. There was nothing the three of us could have done to really change the area. And maybe it wasn't our place, anyway."

With the immediate disturbances dealt with, Sharon and Lily did their best to go back to their normal lives. And it worked, for a while, but something about the house remained unsettling. Eventually, they moved and did what they could to put the experience of the house in Beaverton behind them. Angela told me that even in their new home, Sharon and Lily still feel the presence of Sharon's mother watching over them.

As for the house itself: Sharon's stepfather put the property up for sale, but no buyers would take it, no matter how much he cut the price. Eventually he moved out and, without further explanation, had the house too haunted demolished.

Old Town Pizza

Nina (pronounced Nigh-na) has haunted the building at 226 Northwest Davis Street that now houses Old Town Pizza for over one hundred years. She announces herself with a hint of perfume, a brief glimpse of a black dress, and a lingering presence just over your shoulder, observing the patrons or wandering the basement. Old Town Pizza occupies the original lobby of what was once the Merchant Hotel and is still accented by the hotel's original cast iron beam posts. This cozy, comfortable restaurant has been the location of more than a few sightings over the years, with everyone from the employees to the patrons reporting encounters with the diaphanous Nina. She seems shy during business hours; as the restaurant becomes crowded and busy, she seems to retreat. But early in the morning before opening or as the evening winds down toward close, Nina moves through the restaurant, either minding her own business or interacting with inanimate objects, perhaps in an attempt to make her presence known. Kitchen machinery has come on by itself, chairs move and, late at night, if you listen carefully, it's been said you can hear delicate footsteps creaking across the floorboards of the historic site.

Pictured is Old Town Pizza, home to Nina, a friendly ghost with a sad past.

The Merchant Hotel was built in 1880 by two prosperous lumber barons and, as soon as the doors opened, it became a beacon for Portland's glitterati, men and women dressed in evening clothes and furs filing in and out of the ornate lobby, fine dining on multi-course meals washed down by the best wines and champagnes. The Merchant Hotel became the place to see and be seen. But as is often the case with enclaves of the rich and famous, not all the activities at the Merchant were fit for inclusion in the *Oregonian's* society page. Portland's history of vice is well documented; gambling, rum-running during prohibition, drugs and prostitution, it all flowed beneath the city like a subterranean river of depravity and seeped up through the floor boards to stain the very heights of Portland's high society.

They say she was a prostitute. They say she was sold into the profession just like so many other woman who were trafficked through Portland's notorious Shanghai tunnels, victims of the sex-slave trade, kidnapped and forced into immoral servitude for as long as their owners deemed them profitable or for as long as they stayed alive. Nina is a beautiful name, it's Spanish and, though the pronunciation is unusual, it means simply "girl." It's easy to imagine a beautiful woman to go with a name like that. It conjures images of grace and charm, and she would have had to have both to cater to the upscale clientele of the Merchant Hotel. We don't know how old she was when she was captured and sold any more than we know how old she was when she was murdered. But we do know, purely from the circumstances of her final days, that her life couldn't have been a happy one.

According to the legend, Nina came in contact with a pair of traveling missionaries who had come to Portland to save the city from its multitudinous sins. They promised to help Nina escape her life of forced prostitution, promised to protect her and keep her safe, only if she would provide information about the criminal network that held her captive. Nina agreed. Whether she trusted the missionaries or not, she must have been so desperate to change her circumstances that she was willing to risk her life to do it—and that's exactly what it cost her.

It's not known for certain whether she lived at the Merchant Hotel or if she just went there for business. All we know is, it was the last place she was seen alive. Was it a set up? Did somebody find out she'd talked and lured her to the hotel to silence her for good? Or was it simply bad luck? While waiting for the missionaries to emancipate her as promised, did she finally encounter that one, murderous customer who thought no more of taking her life than crushing an insect beneath his heel? The legend tells us only that she was murdered in the hotel and her body dumped down the elevator shaft.

One wall of that shaft is now a back booth in Old Town Pizza. On that wall, scratched into the bricks, is the name "Nina"... It's purported to be her work, a one-word epitaph scrawled by the hand of a dying woman.

Recently, a current employee was working alone in the kitchen after the restaurant had closed. He had his head down, minding his own business, listening to the distant electric hum of the kitchen machinery while he

Could this be the final message from a dying woman? The name "Nina" is scratched in the brick that was once a part of the elevator shaft in the building that now houses Old Town Pizza. *Photo courtesy Old Town Pizza.*

finished up his closing duties. There was no one else in the restaurant. At least he thought so until he heard footsteps clocking through the kitchen, heading right toward him. But when he looked up, he saw no one there. Just the vague shape of a woman, a dress that swept around her ankles as she moved, old-fashioned laced boots, a delicate pale hand. She stopped when she noticed him notice her, then turned and fled. He followed her to a door in the dining area that led down to the basement, but went no further. Old Town Pizza sits atop one of the entrances to the tunnels that run below Portland, the Shanghai Tunnels, and the employee knew enough of their mysterious history to resist the urge to investigate alone.

You can explore the tunnels if you wish. Tours are organized daily and you can even get a slice of pizza and a drink before you go. It's a great place for amateur ghost hunters and history buffs alike to experience one of the most famous tourist attractions in the city. But be warned: if Nina is any indication, the dead do not rest easy beneath the streets of Portland, and there's no telling who, or what, you may encounter if you go down there.

Commodore Grocery

The Commodore Grocery is located at 621 SW 16th Avenue. A small, narrow store about three times as long as it is wide, it's more East Coast bodega than 7/11-era convenience store. The grocery is situated in a corner of the historic Commodore Building; an art deco tower built on the sloping corner of 16th Avenue and Morrison Street just north of downtown. Constructed in 1925, the Commodore Building is an impressive structure, designed by Herman Brookman, a renowned architect originally from New York City who eventually became one of the northwest's most notable builders. The Commodore Building is imposing, and despite the bright colors—the result of a recent paint job—there's something exceedingly gothic about the structure in addition to its art deco adornments. Surrounded by 1970s style cold glass and steel structures, the Commodore has character, a face, and looking at it, you can almost feel a presence.

The grocery is located a few blocks from the office where I used to work and for awhile I would stop in there just about every day to buy cigarettes. One day, after I'd just signed the contract to write

The Commodore Grocery on the first floor of the Commodore Building located on Southwest 16th Avenue.

this book, I walked into the Commodore at my usual time. Robyn Smith was the clerk who worked most afternoons when I would stop in. Robyn was 27-years-old at the time, originally from Michigan, and she was working at the Commodore while saving money for law school. When I walked into the Commodore that day, Robyn asked how it was going and I told her, "Fantastic! I just signed a contract to write a book about ghosts in Portland." That was all I had time to get out before she waved her hands in the air, took a couple of quick, deep breaths, a hesitant step back and said, "Oh my god. Just this morning ..."

She went on to tell me about a strange experience she'd had in the store just a few hours before I walked in.

On the afternoon of March 24, 2006, Robyn was at her normal place behind the counter working the New York Times crossword puzzle and talking to her friend Kendall who'd stopped in on her way to work. The rain in Portland hangs on through March, April, and May, but that day was unseasonably clear and sunny. Kendall and Robyn were talking about that and about their plans for the weekend, when Robyn noticed Kendall kept looking to her left, down the length of the store toward the back where the coolers were. Robyn kept talking until she noticed her friend was beginning to seem a little uncomfortable. Finally, she said, "What are you looking at?"

Kendall whispered, "We're not alone in here."

Robyn leaned over the counter and looked down toward the back, but she didn't see anyone.

The apparition appeared at the back of the store by the coolers. "I'll see her one second, then look away, and when I look back, she's gone."

"Now she's gone," Kendall said. "I'll see her one second, then look away, and when I look back, she's gone. Is there anyone working in the stockroom?"

Robyn said no, there was no one else in the building, and the only way in or out was the front door. Robyn asked Kendall to describe the person she'd seen and this is what she told her:

"She's short, maybe less than five feet. She has on a dirty white jacket or hoodie and she has long, really long dark hair pulled back into a pony tail." Suddenly Kendall turned back toward the coolers and said,

"There she is again!"

But when Robyn leaned over the counter again to look, there was nobody down there. Kendall said that the woman looked Native American to her, that she had a wrinkled, round face, and she kept moving erratically between the shelves and the cooler. Then she'd just disappear.

After an awkward silence, Kendall said she had to get to work, that maybe her eyes had been playing tricks on her, she'd been up late the night before, but Robyn noticed how unsettled her friend looked on her way out. She told me that when she left, Kendall said something about the whole experience just feeling *"wrong."*

All of that sounded good to me. If that wasn't a perfect ghost story, at least it was a place to start. So I told Robyn I'd like to interview her. If she could wait for just a few minutes, I was going to run back to the office and get my tape recorder and notebook. She said she wasn't going anywhere, but for me to hurry, she didn't feel like being in the store alone right then. I told her I would and hurried out.

As soon as I stepped out into the March sunlight, it started to rain, one of those weird rains that fall from a sunny sky. The oldtimers say that means the devil is beating his wife. It was thin and spitting and the drops seemed like long strands of silver, streaking down from the sky and helioscoping in the bright sun, each drop shot through with a tiny rainbow. I hurried back toward the office, but only got a few blocks before a memory hit me, slamming into focus so hard that it stopped me in my tracks. I stood there in the rain and let the scene from several months before play though my mind.

It had been late in the afternoon and predictably I was on my way down to the Commodore for cigarettes. It was winter then and I remembered pulling my hat down over my eyes to keep my glasses dry and pulling my scarf a little tighter around my neck against the cold. When I walked into the Commodore there was no one behind the counter. The owner was in the back in the stockroom and I could hear her moving boxes and cans around. I knew from experience that all I had to do was wait and she would be out when she reached a stopping point. So I waited. I was studying the display behind the register when I caught the hint of motion out of my peripheral vision. I looked down toward the back of the store expecting to see the owner emerging from the stockroom, but there was no one there.

I thought that was strange, maybe she'd come out for a second and then gone back into the stockroom. So I went on waiting until I noticed it again, just a flash of movement at the very edge of my perception. I turned my head slowly and looked back into the store. That's when I saw her—a short woman with a dirty white coat and a long, dark ponytail trailing down her back. She had a round face and I thought she looked either Native American or like an Eskimo. She was moving with a strange kind of jerking motion, almost like she was vibrating, walking back and forth between the shelf with the chips and the cooler. I didn't watch her for long, just a couple of seconds, because something about the sight of her was unnerving. I couldn't put my finger on it, but just watching her for a few seconds, I felt all kinds of negative, upsetting emotions swell up inside of me. I wasn't afraid, or if I was, I didn't know what was scaring me, but for the few seconds I looked at her I felt a weird combination of fear and anxiety and sadness sweep across me.

I looked away, back at the display behind the register, and when I turned back, the woman was gone. I could feel my pulse racing and I was breathing in short hitches. I closed my eyes and tried to get a hold of myself. Did I need a cigarette that bad? Gradually, my breathing calmed and my heart started to slow and I felt a little normalcy returning to me.

Until I saw her again.

She came out of nowhere. I mean, one second she wasn't there and the next she was, kind of blurring into view. I thought she had been crouching down behind the shelves and then popped up and started her jerking march back and forth between the shelves and the coolers. I thought there must be something wrong with her, maybe she was mentally disabled. In retrospect, it's fascinating how my eyes were telling me one thing and my brain was telling me something else; my eyes were telling me she was literally appearing and disappearing, my brain was telling me she was crouching behind the shelves, hiding and revealing herself. My eyes told me she was blurry, amorphous and insubstantial one second and solid the next. My brain told me my eyes were playing tricks on me and, if it upset me so much to look at her, then I should turn away.

So that's what I did. I turned away and focused all my concentration on the wall behind the register.

I drummed my fingers on the counter, counted my breaths and gnawed at the inside of my lip. My hands wanted to shake and, honestly, I felt like crying. Something about the whole thing was so upsetting; waves of negative energy seemed to pour from the apparition at the back of the store and just because I couldn't see her anymore didn't mean I couldn't feel her.

I waited, resisting the urge to look back. What I didn't do was think too much. My mind seemed to skip over the incredible experience entirely and I started thinking about the work I had to do back at the office. I was about to blow the whole thing off, forget about the cigarettes; after all, I could bum one from someone in the office if I had to or I could walk a few blocks and find another store, but I didn't need to stand there and wait any longer.

I was working myself up to leave when once again I noticed movement out of the corner of my eye. I didn't turn to look; I gripped the counter and kept facing forward. Besides, I didn't have to look because I knew what was going on. Something was approaching. That mental proximity alarm started to sound in my head and I could *feel* someone coming closer, straight up the aisle toward me.

When the owner appeared behind the counter, I had to choke back a cry. I guess I stood there for awhile without saying anything, just holding onto the counter and probably grinning like an over-medicated mental patient because after awhile she gave me a kind of confused smile and said, "Cigarettes?"

I got out of there as fast as I could. At the front door, I looked toward the back one more time. I didn't see the woman, but for just a second I thought I saw something else, a smudge, like a mark made by a soft charcoal pencil when you rub your finger across a paper. You know how when you look at a bright light you can still see the traces of it when you look away? It was like that, but instead of glowing and vivid, it was dark, more like the absence of light than anything.

I walked back to the office and immediately started compiling a list of rational explanations for what I'd seen. Obviously, the owner had someone helping her in the store that day, someone who was a little devel-opmentally disabled and who had a strange way of moving, someone who would crouch down behind the shelves and then jump up and skitter back and forth before ducking back down. Obviously. The rest of it, the wave of unsettling emotions that had swept over me, and that strange, black mark that hung in the air, well, that stuff wasn't worth thinking about. Best to forget it, there were plenty of other things to worry about.

And that's exactly what I did with the whole experi-ence: I had decided not to think about it and, I believe, by the end of the work day I'd forgotten most of what I'd seen. I was supposed to go out with some friends that night, but I begged off and cocooned myself on the couch instead. I felt bad, still upset about some-thing elusive, weighed down by a profound sense of wrongness.

Eventually, even that faded and my mind, like of-ten happens with an experience we can't quite figure out, pushed the incident to the bottom drawer of my memory. And that's where it stayed until that day in March. Now, standing a block away from the grocery in the strange pre-spring shower, I was reliving the entire experience as if it had happened only moments before instead of months ago. Hurrying back to the office to get my notebook and tape recorder, I felt that same emotional upheaval, that same "profound sense of wrongness" as before.

I met Robyn at the Commodore Bar next to the grocery later that afternoon. She filled in the details of the story I've related above, but I didn't tell her about my own encounter because I wanted to hear what she had to say uninfluenced by my information. The physical description of what both Kendall and I saw was almost identical: short woman, the erratic movement, the long dark ponytail, the strange sense of powerful, unsettling emotions. There was a slight difference in how we described her clothing; Kendall thought she had on a white coat or a hooded sweatshirt, I thought she was wearing a puffy kind of ski jacket, once white, but stained gray and streaked with grime. I know that the mind will fill in details when memory draws a blank, that's why eye-witness testimony in court cases can be unreliable, and I wondered if that's what both Kendall and I were doing, filling in the blanks.

Robyn also told me that some time in the building's history the bar where we were meeting and the grocery next door had been occupied by a pharmacy. I immediately got a picture of what the place must have looked like: a long wooden counter, maybe a soda fountain, and the staff dressed in the high-necked white smocks favored by pharmacists in the past. Could that have been what the woman was wearing?

Something so anachronistic that both Kendall and I updated her clothing to a time or reference we were more familiar with? I don't know.

I did some research into the history of the building after that. The apartments upstairs had once been a popular place for visiting sailors to flop, there had indeed been a pharmacy on the location, and past and present tenants told more than a few tales of odd and unsettling encounters on the property. There was a "woman in white" who haunted the halls of the building, a thin, distant wail trailing behind her like a cold winter wind, and a disquieting laugh that seemed to echo from the sealed basement under the bar. And, there was something else, something mischievous and unsettling, that nobody wanted to discuss in detail.

Psychic retro cognition is the act of seeing or sensing something from the past. It occurs spontaneously at times, all though it is uncommon. Psychologist Gardner Murphy proposed the theory that most traditional hauntings are actually cases of retro cognition with an individual becoming momentarily displaced in time and witnessing scenes or events from the past. If that's the case, how do you explain the experiential senses that come from an encounter with the supernatural? How do you explain the strong wave of emotion both Kendall and I felt emanating from the apparition in the grocery? If we were simply witnessing a moment from the past replaying in front of us like a grainy old movie, then how could we pick up on the mind and mood of the entity, sorrow or despair or fear or anger? I concluded that there had to be more to it.

What that is, I'm not qualified to say.

"The Lady in the Lake"

Laurelhurst Park is an oasis of bucolic serenity located along busy SE 39th Street and Stark Avenue in Portland. Insulated from the noisy crush of the city by a thick canopy of trees, Laurelhurst Park is twenty-six acres of dramatic landscape based in part on New York's Central Park. The terrain is rich with long, serpentine paths ideal for leisurely strolls, broad meadows perfect for picnicking and afternoon naps in the soft grass, and a three-acre lake that began life as a watering hole for the Jersey cattle owned by two-time Portland Mayor William S. Ladd. The land was acquired in 1911 by the City of Portland, and by 1919 it had been developed into "the most beautiful park on the West Coast". In 2001, Laurelhurst Park became the first city park named to the National Register of Historic Places.

There is a great deal of history associated with Laurelhurst. The park has been home to parties and weddings, dances and celebrations, proposals and breakups. Popular Easter sunrise services were once held there and, for years, the park's lake was home to the regal pageantry of the annual Rose Festival Queen coronation as the queen and her court would drift majestically across the lake on a flotilla of flower-covered boats and rafts.

But the lake in Laurelhurst Park has more stories associated with it than just high school princesses weeping as a trail of soggy crepe paper and rose petals swirled in their wakes: stories you won't read in any travel guide.

On the morning of October 9, 1936, ten-year-old Donald West was playing in the park near the bank of the lake. At about noon, he found something there that seemed out of place: a woman's suit coat and one shoe. Thinking the clothing had been accidentally left behind, he immediately notified park watchman E.J. Dahl. When Watchman Dahl investigated, he found the clothing belonged to Miss Alla Warineth, 45, of Spokane, Washington. In her pockets were eight dollars in cash and three hundred dollars in American Traveler's checks; no small sum for 1936 and not something a person would purposely leave unattended. But where was Miss Warineth?

Watchman Dahl found out when he casually looked out toward the lake. She was there, face down in the water, drowned.

After a member of the harbor patrol and a fireman had retrieved the body and an autoposy was completed, the authorities found no sign of foul play. Her death was ruled a suicide and the questions of what had brought the Washington resident to the lake in Laurelhurst Park and what had driven her to end her life there were left unanswered.

This incident would have remained little more than a sad footnote to the history of Laurelhurst Park if it wasn't for the experience of a lone jogger some fifty years later. According to reports, early one morning the jogger, a recently widowed man of about middle age, was working his way along his usual route through the park. It was still dark and a thin fog clung to the ground where the path sloped down toward the lake. As he passed, he saw a woman standing there, her head down, close to the water, her posture that of someone in careful concentration or silent prayer. The jogger thought it strange that she would be out so early on a cold, damp morning without a jacket, but she didn't seem chilled by the mist, just silent, just still. He was soon past her and thinking about finishing his run and getting home when he heard the splash.

He doubled back. It could have only taken a few seconds for him to cover the ground, but when he reached the lake, he didn't find the woman where he expected. She wasn't in the shallow water near the bank, but further out, face down, as if she'd been drifting there for some time. Maybe she'd passed out and fallen in, maybe she was sick or hurt. Whatever it was, she needed help, and without thinking, the jogger dashed into the frigid water, forcing his way forward until he was submerged up to his neck. The woman was floating right in front of him, but every time he reached for her, she seemed to move just beyond his fingertips. The cold closed a tight fist around his chest; he felt his footing betray him on the slick bottom of the lake and he started to swim. But still the woman stayed just out of his reach. He made a last ditch effort to grab her, bobbing up and down in the water before hurling forward. But when he came down expecting to wrap his arms around the woman, he slammed into nothing but the icy surface of the lake. He thrashed around in the water desperately trying to find the woman, but got only a mouthful of cold water for the effort. She had vanished.

The exhausted jogger dragged himself back to the shore. Torn over whether he should report to the police something he wasn't sure he could explain to himself, he eventually went home.

Could what the jogger encountered have been a residual haunting, a supernatural playback of a traumatic, life-ending event centered on a moment of intense emotion? If it was, could it have been the death of Alla Warineth he witnessed? There's no way to be certain. As Miss Warineth had done with her motivation for coming to Portland and committing suicide now seventy years ago, the lake in Laurelhurst Park keeps its secrets.

White Eagle

Everybody knows the White Eagle is haunted. Ask anyone in Portland to name a haunted hotspot and chances are they'll mention the famous bar on North Russell Street. Its stories are as much a part of Portland ghost lore as any location and have worked their way into the local mythos as much as the Shanghai Tunnels and the gangster-driven pinball wars of the 1950s. As famous as the White Eagle is for its nightly live music and its historic oak back-bar and original ceramic-tiled floors, the bar is perhaps best known for the exploits of three residents—three residents from the past who still make their presence known nearly a century after their deaths.

The legend contradicts the historical record in places but, like any good story, the tale gains the weight of truth with each telling. So here, as it has been passed to me, is the story of the White Eagle haunting…

The White Eagle is now owned by brothers Mike and Brian McMenamin, but before they purchased the bar and folded it into the McMenamin empire, the establishment was owned by another and it is from his tenure that we have the story of Rose, Sam,

The White Eagle Tavern on North Russell Street, one of the most well known haunted spots in Portland. At night, Rose's laughter still rings through the building accompanied by Sam's sad piano playing.

and the unnamed other. The north side of Portland, back around the turn of the century, was a rough and tumble, two-fisted kind of place, with bars and bordellos a plenty and the White Eagle, with its eleven-room hotel upstairs, smack dab in the middle of the vice. Rose was a beautiful, young escort who plied her trade at the White Eagle, entertaining the men who worked along the waterfront. A dime would buy you a dance, but for more you had to talk to the Chinese bouncer who stalked the first floor, scowling and looking for troublemakers. The White Eagle was as famous for its live music then as it is now and, aside from the beautiful women, one of the major draws to the bar was Sam, the reputed "best piano player in the northwest."

Nightly, Rose danced as Sam played the piano for her. How many nights must he have watched her entertaining other men, breathlessly waiting for her to favor him with a smile or a kind word in between customers? You see, Sam had fallen in love with Rose and, silently, he'd made plans for their future together. He would take her away from the White Eagle and the rain in Portland and the rough hands of the wharf workers and the mill men. He would take her to Seattle or San Francisco and they would live off the money he could surely make as a musician there. He would love her and she would love him back and that would be all they would really need to survive.

One Christmas, as a surprise snow fell outside the bar and Sam hammered out a popular tune on the piano waiting for Rose to emerge from the rooms upstairs, the bouncer noticed that Sam was edgy and throwing back shots of rye, one after another, instead of his customary beer. Sam was building up his courage because tonight was the night. He had almost a thousand dollars saved and a Christmas present for Rose. He would give it to her, she would love it, and he would tell her of the 10:15 train and the two tickets he had in his breast pocket, their passports to a new life together.

When the opportunity came, Sam asked Rose if he could see her privately in one of the rooms upstairs. Rose checked with the bouncer who figured, what the hell, it was Christmas – why not? And the two retired.

It didn't go well. Sam presented Rose with her gift, a silver pendant – two monkeys facing each other, their tails entwined to form the shape of a heart. It was expensive, but tacky, and Rose thanked him and dumped it in the drawer with all the other gifts from her suitors. Then, she prepared to give Sam what she believed he'd come for. But Sam blurted out his plan, cradled her face, and told her of his undying love, of how long he'd waited for this moment and the life he'd mapped out for them—and she laughed at him. She *laughed* at him.

Sam pleaded with her to listen, but she just kept on laughing and drove him into a whiskey and shame fueled rage. He began destroying her room, throwing over the furniture, smashing the mirror, and wailing, screaming with anger and disappointment and heartbreak. The bouncer heard the commotion from downstairs and burst into the room to subdue Sam, but, so fierce was the jilted lover's frenzy, that the much larger bouncer was quickly overpowered and was forced to draw his revolver.

The two men struggled for the weapon and, still mad with unrequited passion, Sam tore the pistol from the bouncer's hand and shot him through the head.

He then turned the gun on Rose and, finally, himself. That Christmas brought three deaths to the White Eagle and the tragedy of that night, even now, haunts the bar.

The former owner and his employees have reported a number of sightings, everything from furniture skittering across the floor, ghostly voices, to mysterious shades drifting up and down the stairs.

One employee tells a story of a silver pendant she saw on the floor during a busy night. She was moving through the tightly packed crowd with her arms full of empty glasses when she spotted something shiny being kicked around the floor. She thought it must have been a piece of jewelry lost by one of the customers and, as soon as she dropped off her load of dishes at the kitchen, she returned to the bar to retrieve it. But when she got back to the spot where she'd seen it, she couldn't find the unusual piece of jewelry anywhere. She asked around in the crowd if anyone had lost anything, but no one had. Later, after the bar emptied out and she was cleaning up, she saw it again, this time glinting next to the stage in the back corner of the bar. She said it was a strange charm, large and gaudy, something silver with a heart shape where the chain would have attached. This time, she turned to the bartender to ask if he saw it, too. He didn't, and when she turned back to the stage, the pendant was gone.

The shadows of that tragic evening still linger throughout the White Eagle. Rose is still there. You can see her sometimes or smell her perfume as she moves through the buildings, perhaps still looking for gentlemen to entertain. There have been several reports of her laughter ringing through the rooms upstairs. It's a harsh laugh, derisive and mocking, but it often gives way to the sounds of sorrow and fear as if she's still pleading with Sam to spare her life.

The bouncer is certainly there. He's the angry ghost, as much a bruiser in death as he was in life. One former employee reported being shoved down the stairs, a powerful push sending her down to the basement when no one was behind her. Others have also reported rough treatment at the hands of an invisible assailant. Antique coins have been known to fall from the ceiling, perhaps in payment for past services rendered, and cold spots abound throughout the bar.

And Sam? Apparently he's there, too. Sorrowful piano music has been heard at times, late at night, after the bands have loaded-out and the last of the customers have gone home, his sad song echoing through the White Eagle, an intemporal requiem for the three lives lost there to violence, all in the name of love.

Portland by Gaslight

Between 1:30 and 5:30 p.m. on October 28, 1909, the seven-room, two-story house on northwest Marshall Street occupied by Mr. and Mrs. Sanders and their eleven-year-old grandson Ernest Harps was struck by the first in a series of the most widely witnessed poltergeist manifestations ever recorded in the history of the Northwest. Furniture moved, dishes smashed, doors slammed. Not only did Mr. and Mrs. Sanders and young Ernest witness all of these events, but also three other relatives living in the house at the time and a number of visitors, many of who later signed affidavits attesting to the supernatural events they'd encountered.

In 1909, the population of Portland stood at 207,214, having more than doubled since the turn of the century. The city's economy was still primarily driven by the powerhouse industries of grain, timber, and the railroads. The recently constructed street car system allowed people to travel as far as ten miles in half an hour and structural steel gave builders the ability to span the Willamette River with longer, taller, and lighter bridges. Skyscrapers grew around elevators and skeletons of steel, reaching high above the masonry structures that had defined the nascent city since its birth. Portland had entered its tumultuous adolescence and the population was experiencing the changes and pains associated with the sudden growth spurt.

Around the globe, mankind seemed to be experiencing the same kind of emotional upheaval. William H. Taft had replaced Theodore Roosevelt in the White House as President of the forty-six states, the U.S. military had deposed the president of Nicaragua, Robert E. Perry reached the North Pole, and the Pittsburgh Pirates defeated the Detroit Tigers, four to three, in the first World Series in history to go seven games. The age of reform was well established in the cultural centers of the country, driven by visionaries like W.E.B. DuBois and Emma Goldman, though in many cities, a woman could still be arrested for smoking in public. In Europe, politics and ethnic hatred had already entrenched nations on the murderous path to the most destructive and costly military conflict in human history at the time, World War I.

But in the house on Marshall Street, the inhabitants were concerned with more immediate troubles. The ghostly activities continued for several days, through All Hallow's Eve, with chairs flipping over, pictures flying from the walls, and inexplicable knockings and bangings echoing through the house. Word of the events soon spread through the city and throngs of curiosity seekers filed through the home, many insisting they, too, saw objects move. A number of theories were posed to explain the phenomena: tiny earthquakes, electrical storms, and cosmic rays. At the turn of the century, the line between scientific fact and speculation was thin and easily crossed by a population concerned simultaneously with post-Edwardian reason and old-world superstition. Explanations for the preternatural could be ascribed to everything from the popularly misunderstood power of the recently discovered atom to the mysterious ether that many believed enveloped our planet and stretched to the furthest reaches of the cosmos.

The Sanders family believed the source of the disturbances was closer to home.

"Ernest has always been strange," his grandmother said of the eleven-year old. He was quiet, thoughtful, and "subject to spasms." The manifestations *did* seem to focus around the boy, occurring primarily when he was in the room or nearby, but by all accounts, he did nothing physically to cause the disturbances. Was he a magnet for the poltergeist, an agent unconsciously drawing the spectral entity's wrath to the family home? A doctor visiting the house saw a candlestick telephone hover over a table while Ernest was in the room, then slam down. Plaster rained from the ceiling when the child moved through the house. His uncle had another explanation, saying simply of his nephew, "The devil is in him."

The publicity around the case became so great that it drew the attention of the American Society of Psychical Research. First organized in 1885 with astronomer Simon Newcomb as president, the Society is dedicated to the investigation of extraordinary and unexplained phenomena. Over its one hundred and twenty-five year history, the Society's membership has included some of the most inquisitive minds of their time: renowned psychologist and professor of philosophy William James, physicists Sir William Barret and Sir Oliver Lodge of Cambridge and Oxford, and the physicist and inventor of Xerox, Chester Carlson. Their headquarters, currently located in New York City, includes laboratories, offices, and a one-of-a-kind library stocked with rare books and arcane manuscripts. In 1909, the Society dispatched two researchers, Mr. Thatcher and Dr. Gilbert, to investigate the strange occurences at the Sanders home.

The investigators traveled to Portland and immediately interviewed the family members in the house and the witnesses. It was clear to both men that Ernest was intricately involved with the haunting and they spent several days cross-examining and observing the boy. Then, as the investigation was just beginning, something happened. A rift developed between Mr. Thatcher and Dr. Gilbert. There is no record available to indicate where the breakdown came or why. Was it a matter of procedure? The American Society of Psychical Research had stringent methods in place to quantify their observations and a defined process for regulating their investigations. What could have compelled Dr. Gilbert to break with his colleague and wash his hands of the entire affair? We may never know. Suffice to say that Dr. Gilbert left Mr. Thatcher alone to continue the investigation.

In the end, Mr. Thatcher gathered signed statements from over twenty witnesses not directly involved with the family, confirming they had seen "queer things" in the house on Marshall Street.

Poltergeist is a German word meaning "noisy ghost". It's typically used to describe a spirit that manifests by moving or influencing inanimate objects, like in the Marshall Street incident. In some rare cases like the famous Bell Witch haunting, poltergeists have been known to vocalize and even cause people to levitate. Many parapsychologists consider poltergeist activity to be a kind of involuntary psycho kinesis focused around or even caused by a pubescent child. A preponderance of evidence in the Marshall Street incident points to young Ernest Harps as the obvious agent for the poltergeist.

Ernest was unable to live with his mother at the hotel where she worked as a housekeeper and his father was apparently absent from the boy's life during this incident. Couple that with adolescence, a stressful time for anyone, and we can only imagine the torrent of conflicting emotions the boy must have been experiencing at the time. Emotions perhaps powerful enough to externally manifest themselves either as a magnet for a spectral entity, one that had possibly died in a powerful rage, or as an uncontrolled psychokinetic phenomena.

Eventually, the Sanders and Ernest left the house on Marshall Street and no further reports of supernatural activity were reported by the family. Time is often the only remedy for a poltergeist. Whether the haunted individual grows past the phase of adolescent instability that initially attracts the entity or if the energy required to maintain its malicious manifestation ultimately exhausts the presence or agent, most poltergeists *do* eventually move on. To where is unknown, as mysterious as where they come from.

Cathedral Park

It has happened before, usually late at night, a frantic call is placed to the Portland Police. Terrible screams can be heard coming from the park on the east side of Willamette River in the St. John's neighborhood. A junk-filled, weed-infested wasteland for decades, the area was cleaned up in the 1970s and eventually christened Cathedral Park in 1980 after the 400-foot tall stone pilings that support the 1,207-foot span of the St. John's Bridge. Panicked citizens report horrific cries piercing the night; surely a terrible crime is being committed in the park. But when officers arrive, they find nothing: no attacker, no victim, just the empty park, silent and still beneath the gothic stone arches of the bridge.

But a horrific crime *did* take place there once, a crime so monstrous in it's ferocity that former Portland Chief of Detectives Captain William D. Browne called it, "the most brutal murder I've ever heard of."

On Friday, August 5, 1949, twenty-two-year-old drifter Morris Leland was cruising in a stolen car through the pre-dawn darkness of St. John's neighborhood. A three-time loser, Leland had washed out of the Army, pulled two stretches in the Oregon State

Penitentiary system, and spent the last three years rolling around Oregon subsisting on petty crimes. Leland was a violent man, uneducated and boiling with rage, filling out his resume of depravity with everything from assault with a deadly weapon to attempted rape. Pressure had been building in him lately fueled by ferocious fantasies of domination and control. A powerless, pathetic loser, he'd reached a breaking point.

At a little past four in the morning, fifteen-year-old Thelma Taylor, a student at Roosevelt High, was walking to her friend Janet's house on North Tyler Avenue. They were meeting there before catching the bus to Hillsboro where they were going to pick beans and berries to earn a little extra money. The summer weather was mild with a low of sixty degrees that morning. If Thelma felt any chill as she walked through the dark to her friend's house, her blue sweater would have been enough to hold the cold at bay until she reached her destination. If only she had.

Leland saw her. Alone and vulnerable, Thelma was the victim he'd been waiting for. He lured her to his car, maybe he asked for directions, maybe he told her he was lost and needed help. According to her parents, Thelma was a quiet, inexperienced girl who'd never been "out with boys"; if not gullible, then she was certainly naive. Whatever Leland had said, it was enough to bring the girl closer to him, close enough for him to brandish his six-inch hunting knife and force her into the car. He drove her a short distance until he reached the empty lot that is now Cathedral Park and marched her out into the glade about 1,000 feet from North Edison Street near St. John Avenue. There he attempted to put his long-drawn plan into action.

But Thelma would not cooperate. According to his own confession, Leland tried to rape Thelma a number of times, but with every attempt she would start to scream, scream louder than he'd ever heard anyone scream in his life. Whether it was for fear of discovery or his own sociopathic inability to process another human being's fear, Leland was never able to consummate his nefarious desire. Instead, he held Thelma prisoner there in the weeds, from sunrise Friday to past sunset on Saturday with only the meager lunch she'd packed the day before to eat, so close to passing traffic, so close to possible rescue, keeping her silent with threats of violence, the knife and his superior strength. Holding her hostage with the only power he possessed—the power to terrorize—Leland kept her for over twenty-four hours, his feeble mind unable to formulate a plan for what to do next. He considered letting her go, but he reasoned, "She was a good girl and might tell." So with little more thought than that, at just before 8 a.m., Saturday, August 6, Leland decided to kill Thelma Taylor.

He beat her savagely with a two-foot long, three-inch thick steel bar. He hit her on the arms and the chest, but she started to scream again, this time louder than ever, screaming for her life. So to silence her, Leland smashed the bar across her forehead viciously enough to dislodge a quarter inch fragment of bone from her skull. "That stopped her," he said later. His thirst for violent release unquenched after he bludgeoned her into unconsciousness, he then stabbed her twice, once in the side and once in the chest. With those injuries, Thelma Taylor died.

Less than a week later, Morris Leland was pulled over in yet another stolen car by a Portland patrol officer. He confessed to the murder almost instantly and led police to Thelma's body, brutalized and bruised, mutilated and hidden beneath six rotten logs. He got the chair for his crimes and the world was no poorer for it.

Since then, the stories of the disembodied screams piercing the night around Cathedral Park have worked their way into Portland legend. Many believe it's the voice of Thelma Taylor they hear, the desperate cries of a tortured, terrified little girl echoing through the decades to reverberate in the present. One area psychic claims that it's not Thelma at all who haunts Cathedral Park, but the tormented soul of her attacker, Morris Leland, condemned to wander the scene of his heinous crime for eternity, perhaps in death endlessly experiencing the suffering he so callously inflicted on Thelma Taylor in life.

The Sandman

Just east of the city's center, across the river, before Belmont crosses Martin Luther King, Jr. Blvd. there is a stretch of warehouses shrouded by the overpass of the Morison Street Bridge. The area runs for several blocks, following the line of the railroad tracks. The bridge and off-ramps overhead block the sun most of the day as well as provide shelter from the elements, but it gives the area a subterranean feel, cavernous, hidden and creepy. The area is haunted by Portland's homeless, huddled in doorways or in temporary camps pitched in the undeveloped lots beneath what some locals call "the pass". Some of the inhabitants are transient, moving with the seasons, but others keep residence beneath the pass year round and it is within that community that the tales of the Sandman are most widely circulated.

The railroads have a long history in Portland; they are one of the region's first "pillar" industries, so it's not surprising that numerous accidents, maulings, and deaths have been associated with them. Train crossings have always been dangerous. Neither is it surprising that tales of haunting seem to gravitate toward the railroads. Ghost stories are carried up

The road down to "the pass", the haunting ground of the railroad wraith "The Sandman".

and down the tracks and across the country, packed in with the cargo in the boxcars. Their histories are inextricably linked.

The railroad wraith that many call the Sandman is an apparition that seems to manifest primarily at the train crossing on Belmont between Water Street and Second Avenue, beneath the canopy of concrete, either right where the road crosses the tracks or within several yards. Like the railroad conductor with the lantern looking for his severed head in Texas or the heartbroken mother searching for her children after a fiery collision in New Mexico, many hauntings at railroad crossings around the country seem to have a purpose. The Sandman does not. No one is really sure what he's doing there or why he's doing it.

One version holds that the Sandman was a switchman, and that on one dark night of bad weather and bad visibility, he either got drunk and passed out or simply fell asleep and caused an accident that claimed his life and many others. It's said he is now eternally damned to man the station he neglected in life. Another holds that the Sandman was a traveler who was lured by a woman off the train for the purpose of Shanghaiing or robbery and, when he discovered the trap, ran from his assailants straight into the path of an on-coming freight train.

A recent sighting of the Sandman was related by one of the year round regulars under the pass, an old-timer. He reports he was walking back toward where he bunks down for the night, pushing his cart next to the tracks, coming west toward Belmont, when he looked down about three yards and saw a man standing there, right in the middle of the tracks. He was wearing a long coat and holding his arms straight out at his side, his head tipped back, staring up at the bottom of the bridge. He didn't move. The old man had seen all kinds down there, it took all kinds to be down there, especially at night, so he kept to himself and paid the tall stranger no mind. Until he got closer. Then, he noticed the man's feet weren't touching the tracks. He barely had feet at all, his form kind of tapered off at the ends: his feet trailed off, his hands drifted like fog beyond the sleeves of his coat, his hair seemed to wave around his head like a weak candle flame guttering at the end of a short wick. He wasn't all there.

The oldtimer hurried past, but kept his eye on the apparition as he did. He said the ghost just floated there, as still as death, like he was waiting for something. As the wail of an approaching train's whistle drew near, the whole figure seemed to bend backwards, slowly, almost like a flower closing up as the sun sets, until he was bent entirely, folded in half. And then it was gone.

Another sighting of the Sandman comes from a woman we'll call "Sheryl H." Sheryl tells an account very different from the others. In her encounter, the Sandman wasn't just standing there, just waiting or, as one story goes, checking his pocket watch. He was definitely *doing* something, something horrifying. It was late one night and Sheryl was on her way home. She had her one-year-old son Alex in the car and she was taking a shortcut under the pass to Belmont. Just as she reached the crossing, the alarm bells and flashing lights came to life and the barrier arms lowered in anticipation of a coming train. Sheryl had driven that way a number of times and she knew that the area could be a little sketchy after dark, but she wasn't too worried. After several years in San Francisco and other large cities, she knew how to handle herself. Still, she had a new baby to think about and she was still battling to find the middle ground between conscientious parent and paranoid, over-protective mother. When the crossing gate stopped her car, she decided it wouldn't

The train crossing where the Sandman terrified a mother and her young son.

be silly at all to lock the car doors. And, the second the locks thunked into place, she was glad of it because a man slammed into the hood of her car.

He'd come running from across the tracks, weaving through the barrier, screaming something. He slammed into her hood and splayed across it, pounding his fists and shouting, wild-eyed and frantic. He scared the hell out of her, even more so when she realized the man wasn't angry, he was terrified.

Sheryl started to put her car in reverse and back out, but the man quickly turned his attention from her to something over his shoulder. He rolled off the hood and ran, feet skittering on the wet pavement, watching behind him as he went. When Sheryl followed the man's gaze toward the tracks, she saw the Sandman.

"He looked really tall," she said, "kind of elongated, stretched tall and thin and wearing this long, heavy coat. He was coming straight toward us."

Sheryl said details were hard to pick out, that he "shimmered and flickered," but one thing was for sure, he was moving fast, walking with a long stride, almost too long, and very fast.

"He wasn't looking at us, I think he was chasing the man who ran past."

The figure moved toward the tracks quickly, but when he reached the center, "he just stopped and stood there." And then the train roared past, "right through him."

Fascinated, Sheryl watched until the train passed. When the last car rolled by and the gates rose, she saw no sign of the figure, just the empty tracks and the street in front of her. She quickly pulled through the crossing and hurried little Alex home. As for further sightings of the Sandman, Sheryl has none, because in her own words, "I don't go down there anymore."

If you want to look for the Sandman, it's easy. Everyone knows where he is, just descend down beneath the Morrison Bridge and follow the train tracks. But if you go looking for him, keep off the tracks and be careful who you talk to. Because down beneath "the pass," chances are the Sandman might be looking for you.

The Shanghai Tunnels

All of the tales in the previous chapters and all of the many haunted houses and bars and hotels that weren't included, all of the stories that proliferate across the city, the North Portland Library and the ghostly children of the Jantzen Beach carousel, all of the paranormal societies and haunted tours make one thing patently clear: a supernatural current runs through Portland. Like a subterranean river of lost souls flowing beneath the asphalt and brick, it feeds spirits and wraiths into the streets and buildings of the city like the Columbia feeds the Willamette. Hauntings overflow their banks and inundate the land of the living with every manner of manifestation catalogued by parapsychologists. Portland is saturated with ghosts. But why? What kind of sin brings as its punishment an infestation of phantasms and nightshades; and how can a city atone for an offense that would draw such terrible retribution?

Almost since its incorporation in 1851, Portland has concerned itself with maintaining a façade of Victorian gentility, demonstrating an appearance of civility and restrained manors perhaps out of embarrassment over the region's frontier roots and rough

A barricaded entrance to the Shanghai Tunnels, the source of Portland's secret shame and home to countless hauntings.

and tumble sensibility. Through its early history, Portlanders wanted to be viewed as slightly more refined and cultured than their neighbors to the north and south, Seattle and San Francisco, and at least above the contempt of those taste-makers in the east and across the Atlantic.

Abroad, unfortunately, the Rose City's reputation wasn't quite as chaste or unsullied as the residents would have liked. As a matter of fact, it was considered positively scandalous in places, called "The Un-Heavenly City" by some in the far east, and not entirely without justification. This city's hands have never been wholly clean of mud or blood.

It's 1868 and you're a soldier home from the war or a sailor shipping into port and looking for a drink and a good time. Or it's 1907 and you're a ranch hand in town to blow your stake on a little whiskey and a little company. Maybe it's 1923 and you're a young woman from a tiny farm community in eastern Oregon and you've come to the big city with stars in your eyes and dreams of a dancer's life, any of those or more. Whatever way, you're in Portland and you stop by a joint with a name like Erickson's Saloon or The Snug Harbor, maybe Valhalla or a pool hall or gambling den. Or maybe you're just walking down the street minding your own business, looking for an address in Old Town, and you meet a friendly man who doesn't know anybody in the city either and wants to buy you a drink. So you go. And your life is never the same again. That is, if you live.

You've fallen into the clutches of a "crimp" and before the night is over you will be drugged, robbed, dropped down a trapdoor called a "deadfall" in the back of a building or right in the middle of the opium den, and descend into a labyrinthine hell where you will be caged, assaulted, and sold. At best, it's only your forced labor your new master seeks; at worst, it's something infinitely more precious.

This form of institutionalized kidnapping in Portland got the nickname "Shanghaiing" and took place with the tacit collusion of the police, politicians and businessmen along the waterfront and through the city from 1850 until 1941. Most of the men were taken to work on ships headed toward the Pacific. A sea captain would pay a crimp (basically a hired thug) fifty to fifty-five dollars a head to crew up his vessel. The crimp would drug the cowboy or logger and have them spirited away through narrow brick and stone basement passages that became known as the Shanghai Tunnels, forced into cramped, crowded cells and cages, and held until the ship was set to make way, often not for several days. They were drugged again for transport through the tunnels and to the docks, not to wake up until after the ship was deep into the waters of the Pacific. It could take six years for a man to find his way home, if he ever made it at all.

Women were taken from the dance halls and off the streets in much the same way and for much the same reason. They were crew, but instead of working the rigging of a schooner, they were forced to staff the hotels and brothels that financed and serviced the criminal syndicate, held prisoner by drugs and threats of violence rather than the remoteness of the sea, but prisoners all the same. Any attempt at escape could cost a woman her life or worse, like Nina when she sought deliverance from the Merchant Hotel. Even death hasn't provided her freedom and she's held prisoner there still.

At the height of the Shanghai trade, 1,500 souls were taken a year, men and women kidnapped and enslaved and often killed. It was dangerous business and the crimps weren't terribly concerned about their victim's wellbeing or the safety of the knockout drugs they used. Men and women died from drug overdoses, smothered or starved to death in the cells beneath the city, some were simply murdered when no one wanted to buy them. Over a hundred years, there must have been thousands who died in the tunnels.

The tunnel system is massive, stretching along the waterfront and into town, winding through cellars and passageways as far west as Northwest 24th Street, connecting such Portland icons as the Crystal Ballroom and Ringler's Annex to China Town. Plenty of room for wandering spirits.

At one time during Portland's prohibition-era racketeering renaissance, barrels of whiskey were reportedly stored in the secret passageways. The tunnels provided an excellent distribution channel between the speakeasies. They also made handy escape routes and at least one gangland massacre is said to have taken place in the tunnels. Details are scarce, but the story tells of a raid at one of the businesses connected by the same stretch of tunnel running from Ringlers' on Stark Avenue to the Crystal Ballroom on Burnside Street. Panicked patrons and desperate gangsters alike rushed into the underground passageways. But it wasn't the police they were fleeing; it was a rival gang of hitmen masquerading as Portland's finest, armed with Tommie guns and fire axes. They pursued the fleeing crowd into the tunnels, chasing them as far as Washington, until their terrified prey reached the bottle-neck of a narrow archway and the killers laid into the throng with lead and steel.

Today, a café and bar called Scooter McQuades occupies the building over the site of the massacre and, according to long-time regular customers and some reluctant-to-talk employees, to this day it's plagued by an angry apparition – or several. A vaporous glow, only vaguely human-shaped, emerges from the basement and tears through the bar, brushing past patrons in a

rush to get to the door. Sometimes, it looks like one being, others it looks like more, a group, rushing in a mass, bumping chairs and knocking over drinks.

Another view of the tunnels. How many lives were lost down there? How many souls are still trapped beneath the city's streets?

One regular customer and an employee finally decided to investigate. One night, just before the time when the specter would usually make its mad dash through the building, they descended into the dark basement armed only with flashlights and a curiosity that, temporarily, outweighed their apprehension. The light fixtures didn't work beyond the top landing, no one from the bar bothered to go further than that, so the flashlights had to be enough for them to navigate their way down the steep, wooden stairs. When they reached the dirt floor, the dim circles of light picked out dusty and broken artifacts from the past: a three-legged chair, a smashed mirror, and a boarded-up, chained archway, a tunnel entrance that pointed back toward Ringler's.

The wood blocking the tunnel was cool to the touch, the ancient padlock on the chain too cold to handle. It had been sealed for decades, maybe longer, and some of the tunnels in that part of town had collapsed and were impassible. But they heard something on the other side of the barricade. They pressed their ears against the cold wood and listened and what they heard sounded like more than the wind—it was a moan, long and drawn out, building toward a wail like "a human fog horn." They listened for as long as they could, until they realized the sound wasn't building in intensity, it was moving closer.

Something was rumbling through the sealed passageway, coming right toward them, not just a wall of sound, but a wall of panic, waves of it, a massive expression of terror rushing through the tunnel. They turned and ran for the stairs and just made the top

Scooter McQuades is located over the site of a purported gangland massacre.

before the torrent of glowing specters made their mad dash for escape, up from the basement and through the building toward the front door, but not quite making it. Like always, the forms dissipated a few feet from the exit, their cries trailing off until they were lost beneath the sounds of traffic on Washington.

This incident was the most active encounter ever experienced at Scooter McQuades, even the participants pointed that out, but to this day reports of ghostly encounters can be heard, not only there, but at all the buildings that connect to that section of the tunnel.

Mass hauntings are not rare in the Shanghai Tunnels. Often it's not just one spirit but many trapped beneath the ground, either a random collection of phantoms who died at different times under different circumstances gravitating to a single location or, like on Washington Street, a group of ghosts all ensnared in a single point of time, an eternal tape loop perpetually replaying the moment of death.

Though spread throughout the city, perhaps the greatest concentration of lost souls are localized around the tunnels nearest the river. This is where the majority of Shanghaied victims were held and where most of the deaths occurred. The most tragic incident related to the haunting of the tunnels took the lives of up to one hundred men in a single night and it's with this tale that we close: the wreck of the *Jennifer Jo*.

The *Jennifer Jo* was a four-masted schooner that, in 1902, was commanded by a captain so vile and cruel, so violent and ruthless in his pursuit of profit and social gain, that he became known as "Captain Death" for the high mortality rate of his crew. Shipping out on the *Jennifer Jo* was, at best, a guarantee of several years of pain and suffering that would leave a man broken and bankrupt and, at worst, a death sentence. When the ship pulled into port that May of 1902, nearly two-thirds of the crew had abandoned ship or perished beneath the waves of the Pacific. Captain Death needed men, and in Portland, he knew just where to get them. An army of crimps was dispatched that night with orders to bring the *Jennifer Jo* as many men as she could hold.

The crimps moved through the bars and gambling dens of the city, through the back alleys and abandoned buildings, along the waterway and the hotels, drugging, clubbing and dragging men through the deadfalls, indiscriminately capturing and kidnapping anyone they possibly could that night, driven by greed to work extra hard. Sailors, soldiers, farm boys, city dwellers, anyone the crimps could corner or con fell victim to Captain Death's call for a crew.

So many men were shanghaied that the cells and walkways underground became stuffed beyond capacity. Some were held for over forty-eight hours, pressed into their cages so tightly that they were unable to sit down or even breathe. Bones were broken in the miserable conditions and more than a few men died, deprived of oxygen as more and more bodies were forced into the cages. When food was finally provided, the starving men wolfed down the thin gruel and stale bread, unaware it was laced with the same knock out drug that had led to their capture. Once the men were unconscious, they were spirited through the tunnels like cord wood to the waiting *Jennifer Jo*.

A narrow passage through the tunnels leading toward the waterfront, a "raging river of the dead."

The *Jennifer Jo* never made it to sea. Some say she struck something in the water, a log, maybe a rock or another vessel. Maybe the hand of fate simply decided to end Captain Death's nefarious career, reached up from the depths and dragged the ship down. Some say she broke up and some say she capsized, strange for such a well-traveled waterway, but the ship vanished beneath the waves with all hands aboard. Most of the shanghaied men would have still been unconscious; the strength of the drug was calculated to insure that the victims didn't awake until after they were well on their way. Packed below decks and asleep, they didn't stand a chance. Perhaps the icy cold of the water roused some of them, but it would have been too late—they would have woken just in time to realize they were drowning, their lungs filling with frigid water as they sank into the darkness... over one hundred men.

The date of the wreck of the *Jennifer Jo* is difficult to pin down, but in a number of stories I've heard, the tellers mentioned the disaster occurring on the eve of St. George's Day. In England, St. George's Day is celebrated on April 23, but for the Eastern Orthodox churches the date is May 6. And in the country of Georgia, the date is November 23. It is also said in many Balkan countries that when the clock strikes midnight on the eve of St. George's Day "all the evil things in the world will have full sway."

The story goes that the kidnapped men of the *Jennifer Jo* return every year to the tunnels on the date of the disaster, sodden specters roaming the passageways seeking revenge. They've been heard, they've been seen, and a few people have reported feeling a wet hand drop down on their shoulder as they worked their way through the tunnels.

I decided to investigate the tunnels and signed up for one of the underground tours. There are different tours in town provided by a couple of different companies. Just search the Internet for "Shanghai Tunnels, Portland, Oregon" and you can find all the information you need. There are tours that focus on the hard and fast history of the tunnels and there are tours that concentrate on the haunted aspects of underground Portland. Both are fun and informative, depending on where your interests lie. Surprisingly enough, I *didn't* take the ghost tour, for reasons I'll make clear in a moment.

Since beginning work on this book, I've used a number of sources for supernatural information. I have interviewed witnesses, friends of witnesses, local historians, business owners, and ghost enthusiasts. I've read books and magazines and spent endless hours prowling the Internet. But in all that time, no single source has provided the kind of invaluable assistance as the one I relied on for these next few pages.

Not long after starting the first chapters, I was in the Basement Pub on Southeast 12th Street. The Basement is a few blocks from my home and I'd say about a third of this book was physically written there and even more was fretted over. I was holding forth with my newly discovered ghost lore knowledge, relating tales of phantom dogs and haunted department stores for the regulars, trying to impress the pretty bartender, when I noticed a lone figure sitting at the end of the bar. He was a tall man, well over six feet, lanky-thin with long, frizzy gray hair and a wide-brimmed felt hat pulled low over his eyes. He kept his head down and his hands cupped around his beer. When I finished my story, he looked up, leveled his gaze at me, his gray eyes glistening in the candlelight, and said, "So you think you know about ghosts."

This was my introduction to Latimer Hessman.

Latimer Hessman is somewhere between forty-five and two hundred years old, he would never tell me his age. He isn't from Oregon, but he has lived here for over twenty-five years. He doesn't talk a lot, he listens; but when he does talk, what he has to say is both fascinating and disturbing—and haunting.

Latimer Hessman saw his first ghost when he was seven years old. His family lived in the country on a dairy farm over an hour's drive from the nearest town. His days were filled with work, even at that young age, helping his mother and grandmother and aunt with everything from house chores to difficult physical labor. They had no television and the radio in his grandmother's parlor seemed to receive only religious programs, real fire and brimstone fare, apparently broadcast from not only several states away, but also several decades in the past. The only books in the home were the Bible and a collection of Jonathan Edwards' Calvinist sermons. His primary source of recreation was the old tire swing that hung from a crooked tree around the side of the house. For the short time between the end of the workday and the start of supper, Latimer would slide into that tire and swing as hard and as high as he could, back and forth, as the evening sky darkened from the dull brown of a fresh bruise to purple to black, back and forth until he rocked himself into a trance, or to what Latimer calls "the other place."

He saw the boy Disty on a cold autumn evening as he swung under the creaking branch of the old tree. He said the boy was just standing there, about three yards away, watching him on the swing, dressed in a checkered work shirt and dark jeans rolled into cuffs, his hair buzzed down to a fine fuzz, and his head cocked to the side, his neck bent at a ninety-degree angle so his left ear almost touched his shoulder. Latimer wasn't scared; he was too deep into the meditative serenity of his other place to be anything but curious. The two boys simply looked at each other until Latimer's mother called him in to supper. At the sound of her voice, the boy vanished or "dist-appeared" as he later told his mom.

From then on, every night, as Latimer played on the swing, his strange companion joined him, moving slowly closer over time until, eventually, he stood only a foot or two away. Then he began to speak.

"He told me things," Latimer said, "things that made me see the world in a different way. Our world and theirs."

Through all of our conversations, Latimer Hessman was reluctant to talk about his strange gift. He doesn't have a website and he doesn't advertise his ability, but one thing was clear from our talks—Latimer Hessman sees the dead and it's not something he looks on as a blessing. I think the only reason he spoke to me that first night was because I amused him. But after that first conversation I knew I had a precious

111

source and I never let up on him, asking his opinion and drilling him to verify local stories. When it came time to investigate the Shanghai Tunnels, I knew I had to have Mr. Hessman accompany me.

It took a great deal of cajoling and begging and more than a few beers, but he finally agreed, but on strict conditions. First off, he didn't want to take the ghost tour; he didn't want to be influenced by the experiences of others. Second, we could tell no one what we were doing there; we had to go undercover, just two tourists walking through the tunnels. And third, when I wrote the book, I couldn't use his real name. I agreed to all three, and within a week, we met at Old Town Pizza and joined up with a group for the tour.

During our time underground I took the photos included in these pages and listened to our guide. Latimer hung back away from the rest of the group and, the few times I tried to catch his eye, I saw that they were unfocused and slightly glazed, staring off at things the rest of us didn't see. I enjoyed the tour, but when we emerged I couldn't shake a strong, strange feeling of disquiet. My emotions felt raw, drawn to the surface, uncomfortably reminiscent of the feelings I had in the Commodore Grocery. Latimer and I retired to the Basement Pub and I activated my tape recorder to capture his impressions.

"They're down there," he said. "They're all still down there."

I asked him if he meant the shanghaied men from the *Jennifer Jo* and he said, "Yes, but that's not all. It's the kidnapped, it's the crimps, 'The Wrath of God burns against them, their damnation does not slumber

… the flames do now rage and glow.' Everybody, it's a conduit, a vortex, a raging river of the dead."

He was obviously upset, drawn and drained, and I was reluctant to push him for further details but I wanted just a little more, so I asked him, "What did you see down there?"

Latimer Hessman looked at me with those strange, gray eyes and said in the slightly amused, slightly annoyed tone you'd use with someone incapable of understanding a painfully obvious point, "Ghosts."

Do It Yourself Ghost Hunting

"... the communication
Of the dead is tongued with fire beyond
the language of the living."
- *T.S. Eliot*

What would you say to a ghost if you met one? What do you think they might have to say to you? Would you have the courage to approach an apparition if one materialized right in front of you? What if they approached you?

There's no way to answer those questions, not really, until you're in the situation. Hypothetically, it's easy for us to say, "I ain't afraid of no ghost." I've said it, usually in a safe environment with friends around and the sun in the sky. But right now, as I write this, alone at night with the winter wind blowing sheets of rain against my office window and the old tree outside scratching its skeletal branches on the roof like fingernails on a coffin lid, I can't be so sure. The storm is pretty fierce, what if the lights go out? What if I find myself suddenly alone in the dark and, as I sit here waiting for my pupils to dilate, I hear something dragging itself up the stairs? Am I going to stand up and say, "Tell me? Tell me what it's like on the other side!" Or will I squeak out a pitiful squeal like a mouse on helium and dash for the relative safety of the blankets on my bed?

Hard to say. But if you are wondering how you would perform in the presence of the supernatural, if you're curious to find out if your fear and trepidation might take a back seat to a sense of wonder and awe, then maybe it's time for you to test your mettle and go out on your very own ghost hunt.

To begin with, we need to draw the distinction between a ghost hunt and a paranormal investigation. True investigations follow a strict set of guidelines. They follow the scientific method and are generally undertaken by trained experts with specialized equipment; you can find out more about the methods and tools of ghost investigators in the appendix of this book. A ghost hunt is something anyone can do. It's a fun activity for friends with an interest in the supernatural and a fascinating pastime enjoyed all around the world. Of course, you don't want to just jump in without at least some information about what to do and what to expect.

To begin with, you need to select your location. You'll want to do some research first. Listen to local ghost legends to find the most potentially haunted site, like many of the places in this book, then check historical records at the library and on the Internet to arm yourself with as much information as possible. Who owns the property now? Who owned it before? Do you need permission to investigate the site or is it open to the public? If so, make sure you know the hours of operation. It's tempting to go to a location when no one else is around, but you don't want to break the law.

Next, select the equipment you want to take with you on your hunt. You'll want a camera, certainly, to catch any manifestations or globes, and a tape recorder to keep an oral log of your adventures and to capture any strange sounds you might hear. You'll also want a notebook and a pen to jot down notes and impressions, and an outdoor thermometer to measure any anomalous changes in temperature. A cold spot is a good indicator that something supernatural may be near. If you can, take a video camera with night vision capabilities. Many consumer grade cameras come equipped with this feature now and that could certainly give you an advantage in recording an event invisible to the human eye. Of course, you'll want to bring along a flashlight and fresh batteries. Candles are good, too, especially for setting the ghost-hunting mood, but be very careful with any open flame.

Once you have your equipment and your location secured, establish a base of operations at the site. This should be your group's rallying point, a place to start from and a place to meet up once the hunt is complete. Many believe that spirit activity is greatest just before and immediately following sunset, so carefully observe your location at that time and take photos and measurements. Once the sun goes down, your group should spend some time in silent meditation, clearing their thoughts and opening their mind's eyes. Once the group is ready, have your members fan out through the location in groups of at least two. Whatever you do, don't let anyone go off alone. You never know what might happen. Once the hunt is completed, have your group gather again to compare notes.

Most importantly, have fun. And always remember to be respectful to those around you, both the living and the dead.

Glossary

(The following section is provided by the Chester County Paranormal Research Society in Pennsylvania and appears in training materials for new investigators. Please visit www. ChesterCountyprs.com for more information.)

Air Probe Thermometer

A thermometer with an external probe that is capable of taking instant measurements of the air temperature.

Anomalous field

A field that cannot be explained or ruled out by various possibilities, which can be a representation of spirit or paranormal energy present.

Apparition

A transparent form of a human or animal, a spirit.

Artificial field

A field that is caused by electrical outlets, appliances, etc.

Aural Enhancer

A listening device that enhances or amplifies audio signals. i.e., Orbitor Bionic Ear.

Automatic writing

The act of a spirit guiding a human agent in writing a message.

Base readings

The readings taken at the start of an investigation and used as a means of comparing other readings taken later during the course of the investigation.

Demonic Haunting

A haunting that is caused by an inhuman or subhuman energy or spirit.

Dowsing Rods

A pair of L-shaped rods or a single Y-shaped rod, used to detect the presence, often water or an anomalous field.

Electro-static generator

A device that electrically charges the air often used in paranormal investigations/research as a means to contribute to the materialization of paranormal or spiritual energy.

ELF

Extremely Low Frequency.

ELF Meter/EMF Meter

A device that measures electric and magnetic fields.

EMF

Electro Magnetic Field.

EVP

Electronic Voice Phenomena.

False positive

Something that is being interpreted as paranormal within a picture or video and is, in fact, a natural occurrence or defect of the equipment used.

Gamera

A 35mm film camera connected with a motion detector that is housed in a weatherproof container and takes a picture when movement is detected. Made by Silver Creek Industries.

Geiger Counter

A device measuring gamma and x-ray radiation.

Infra Red

An invisible band of radiation at the lower end of the visible light spectrum. With wavelengths from 750 nm to 1 mm, infrared starts at the end of the microwave spectrum and ends at the beginning of visible light. Infrared transmission typically requires an unobstructed line of sight between transmitter and receiver. Widely used in most audio and video remote controls, infrared transmission is also used for wireless connections between computer devices and a variety of detectors.

Intelligent haunting

A haunting of a spirit or other entity that has the ability to interact with the living and act to make its presence known.

Milli-gauss

Unit of measurement, measures in 1000th of a gauss and is named for the famous German mathematician, Karl Gauss.

Orbs

Anomalous spherical shapes that appear on video and still photography.

Pendulum

A pointed item that is hung on the end of a string or chain and is used as a means of contacting spirits. An individual will hold the item and let it hang from the fingertips. The individual will ask questions aloud and the pendulum answers by moving.

Poltergeist haunting

A haunting marked by violent outbursts with doors and windows slamming shut, items thrown and objects knocked off of surfaces. Poltergeist hauntings are usually focused around a specific individual who lives or works at the location and who must often be present for the activity to occur. A poltergeist haunting may be caused by a human agent or spirit/energy that may be drawn to the agent or location.

Portal

An opening in the realm of the paranormal that is a gateway between one dimension and the next. A passageway for spirits to come and go through. See also Vortex.

Residual haunting

A haunting that is an imprint of an event or person that plays itself out in a loop until the energy that causes it has burned itself out.

Scrying

The act of eliciting information with the use of a pendulum from spirits.

Table Tipping

A form of spirit communication where tables are used as a tool to initiate contact. Individuals will sit around a table and lightly place their fingertips on the edge to elicit responses from a spirit. The Spirit will respond by "tipping" or moving the table.

Talking Boards

A board used as a means to communicate with a spirit. Also known as a Quija Board.

Vortex

A whirling mass that draws everything near it towards its center.

White Noise

A random noise signal that has the same sound energy level at all frequencies.

Equipment

In this section, the Chester County Paranormal Research Society looks at the application and benefits of equipment used on investigations with greater detail. The equipment used for an investigation plays a vital role in the ability to collect objective evidence and helps to determine what *is* and *is not* paranormal activity. But a key point to be made here is: the investigator is the most important tool on any investigation. With that said, let us now take a look at the main pieces of equipment used during an investigation...

The Geiger Counter

The Geiger counter is device that measures radiation. A "Geiger counter" usually contains a metal tube with a thin metal wire along its middle. The space in between them is sealed off and filled with a suitable gas and with the wire at about $+1,000$ volts relative to the tube.

An ion or electron penetrating the tube (or an electron knocked out of the wall by X-rays or gamma rays) tears electrons off atoms in the gas. Because of the high positive voltage of the central wire, those electrons are then attracted to it. They gain energy that collide with atoms and release more electrons, until the process snowballs into an "avalanche," producing an easily detectable pulse of current. With a suitable filling gas, the flow of electricity stops by itself, or else the electrical circuitry can help stop it.

The instrument was called a "counter" because every particle passing it produced an identical pulse, allowing particles to be counted, usually electronically. But it did not tell anything about their identity or energy, except that they must have sufficient energy to penetrate the walls of the counter.

The Geiger counter is used in paranormal research to measure the background radiation at a location. The working theory in this field is that paranormal activity can effect the background radiation. In some cases, it will increase the radiation levels and in other cases it will decrease the levels.

Digital and 35mm Film Cameras

Digital cameras have been at the center of much debate in the field of paranormal research over the years.

The earlier incarnations of digital cameras were plagued with problems in the realm of paranormal investigation and notorious for creating "false positive" pictures. A "false positive" picture is a picture that has anomalous elements within the image that are the result of a camera defect or other natural occurrence. Many paranormal investigators rely on traditional thirty-five millimeter photography.

Video Cameras

The video camera is also a fundamental tool in the investigation as another way for collecting objective evidence that can support the proof of paranormal activity. The video camera can be used in various ways during the investigation. It can be set on a tripod and left in a location where paranormal activity has been reported. It can also be used as a hand-held camera and the investigator will take it with them during their walk through investigation as a means of documenting to hopefully capture anomalous activity on tape. Infra-Red technology has become a feature on most consumer level video cameras and depending on the manufacturer can be called "night shot" or "night alive." What this technology does is allow us to use the camera in zero light. Most cameras with this feature will add a green tint or haze to the camera when it is being used in this mode. A video camera with this ability holds great appeal to the paranormal investigator.

EMF/ELF Meters

EMF = Electro Magnetic Frequency   ELF = Extremely Low Frequency

The EMF/ELF meter is a device that measures Electric and Magnetic fields in an AC or DC current field. It measures in a unit of measurement called "milli-gauss," named for the famous German mathematician, Karl Gauss. Most meters will measure in a range of 1-5 or 1-10 milli-gauss. The reason that EMF meters are used in paranormal research is because of the theory that a spirit or paranormal energy can add to the energy field when it is materializing or is present in a location. The theory says that, typically, an energy that measures between 3-7 milli-gauss may be of a paranormal origin. This doesn't mean that an artificial field can't also measure within this range. That is why we take base readings and make maps notating where artificial fields occur. The artificial fields are a direct result of electricity, i.e. wiring, appliances, light switches, electrical outlets, circuit breakers, high voltage power lines, sub-stations, etc.

The Earth emits a naturally occurring magnetic field all around us and has an effect on paranormal activity. Geo-magnetic storm activity can also have a great influence on paranormal activity. For more information on this kind of phenomena visit: *www. noaa.sec.com*.

There are many different types of EMF meters; and each one, although it measures with the same unit of measurement, may react differently. An EMF meter can range from anywhere to $12 to $1,000 or more depending on the quality and features that it has. Most meters are measuring the AC (alternating current, the type of fields created by man-made electricity) fields and some can measure DC (direct current-naturally occurring fields, batteries also fall into the category of DC) fields. The benefit of having a meter that can measure DC fields is that they will automatically filter out the artificial fields created by AC fields and can pick up more naturally occurring electro magnetic fields. Some of the higher-tech EMF meters are so sensitive that they can pick up the fields generated by living beings. The EMF meter was originally designed to measure the earth's magnetic fields and also to measure the fields created by electrical an artificial means.

There have been various studies over the years about the long-term effects of individuals living in or near high fields. There has been much controversy as to whether or not long-term exposure to high fields can lead to cancer. It has been proven though that no matter what, long term exposure to high fields can be harmful to your health. The ability to locate these high fields within a private residence or business is vital to the investigation. We may offer suggestions to the client as to possible solutions for dealing with high fields. The wiring in a home or business can greatly affect the possibility of high fields. If the wiring is old and/or not shielded correctly, it can emit high fields that may affect the ability to correctly notate any anomalous fields that may be present.

Audio Recording Equipment

Audio recording equipment is used for conducting EVP (Electronic Voice Phenomena) research and experiments. What is an EVP? An EVP is a phenomenon where paranormal voices or sounds can be captured with audio recording devices. The theory is that the activity will imprint directly onto the device or tape, but has not been proven to be an absolute fact. The use of an external microphone is essential when conducting EVP experiments with analog recording equipment. The internal microphone on an analog tape recorder can pick up the background noise of the working parts within the tape recorder and can taint the evidence as a whole. Most digital recorders are quiet enough to use the internal microphone, but as a general rule of thumb, we do not use them. An external microphone will be used always. Another theory about EVP research is that an authentic EVP will happen within the range 250-400hz. This is a lower frequency range and isn't easily heard by the human ear, and the human voice does not emit in this range. EVP is rarely heard at the moment it happens—it is usually revealed during the playback and analysis portion of the investigation.

Thermometers

The use of a thermometer in an investigation goes without saying. This is how we monitor the temperature changes during the course of an investigation. CCPRS is currently using digital thermometers with remote sensors as a way to set up a perimeter and to notate any changes in a stationary location of an investigation. The Air-probe thermometer can take "real time" readings that are instantly accurate. This is the more appropriate thermometer for measuring air temperature and "cold spots" that may be caused by the presence of paranormal phenomena.

Index